A Christian Guide for Reflection
and Discussion

A Christian Guide for Reflection and Discussion

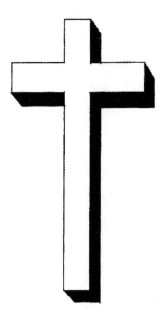

DISCUSSION IS THE ROAD TO LEARNING
This Course could be Sponsored by a Church or Individual Christians.

<u>A Workbook</u>

by Corbin M. Wright – MRE from
New York Theological Seminary

authorHOUSE®

AuthorHouse™
1663 Liberty Drive
Bloomington, IN 47403
www.authorhouse.com
Phone: 1-800-839-8640

Published by AuthorHouse   06/17/2013

ISBN: 978-1-4772-9956-2 (sc)
ISBN: 978-1-4772-9955-5 (e)

CONTENTS

Over 200 Questions are posed for you here on all these topics for your Reflection and Discussion which are <u>all</u> the questions Christians need to consider in their daily lives.

IF THERE ARE ANY COMMENTS ONE CAN WRITE TO <u>CORBIN M. WRIGHT,</u> GREADUATE OF NEW YORK THEOLOGICAL SEMINARY <u>corbinw@hotmail.com</u>

Dedicated to my one and only

Lord and Savior

Jesus Christ

THREE APPROACHES ON HOW TO USE THESE QUESTIONNAIRES

THE FIRST APPROACH ON HOW TO USE THESE QUESTIONAIRES.

These questionnaires should be taught in the order in which they appear in the book with the one on Evangelism being the first, because this is really the foundation of all the other questions contained therein; and they should be taught without skipping any of the topics because to fully understand Christianity you need to delve into all these subjects. Now I'm going to suggest three approaches that one can use in dealing with these questionnaires.. The first approach, and probably the easiest to organize, could be a 10 week Bible course: One questionnaire (only questions of interest) per class. Of course before the 10 week Bible course begins you should have an introductory class to indicate to the participants how you're going to teach the course. Now if you don't cover all the questions that the participants are interested in with some of the questionnaires the first time around, you could go around a second time with those questionnaires and cover those missing questions of interest.

THE SECOND APPROACH ON HOW TO USE THESE QUESTIONNAIRES

A second way one could use this questionnaire guide would be by developing "a Philips 66" approach, if you're not going to use these questionnaires in a Bible class. That is, at a convenient time, such as, after your Sunday morning worship service when you have most of your people present, hold your discussion group by, if you have more than 8 attending, breaking them up into smaller groups. Each group would then select a leader and a recording secretary, after which you would ask each group to discuss the same question or questions (see below for suggestive questions) for 15 to 30 minutes. You would then bring the groups back together again into a larger whole so that the recording secretaries could report on what went on in the smaller groups. And finally, you would conclude with any further discussion needed by the larger whole. The complete procedure should last about one hour. The questionnaires should serve as reference points toward some of the questions that might come up during the smaller group discussions. If you find the time too short in discussing the theme for the day, you can always set up an additional hourly discussion group a little bit later on the same topic.

Some suggestive questions for each class or group could be:

Chapt 1   How do you communicate your faith? Is it effective? How could it become more effective?

Chapt 2   Why do good people have to suffer, and how can you deal with this problem?

Chapt 3   Economic Suffering-How can one find a job? How can one become Financially Independent?.

I'm writing this book because I organized a single topic discussion "Predestination" in my church many years ago and it proved quite successful in that the people requested a second discussion on the same topic. I feel this can be done with any topic Christians are concerned about.

AND THE THIRD APPROACH ON HOW TO USE THESE QUESTIONNAIRES

And the final approach could be that during the first class each participant should read the questionnaire thoroughly, if they haven't already done so, and then have them choose the three most important questions contained within that particular questionnaire that they would like to see discussed. And then designate these questions as #1, #2, and #3. Then have one of the participants, who is systematically chosen, select their question #1 that he or she would like to see discussed, and then have that person lead a discussion, using Scripture where possible, on that question within the group. Then when that discussion is exhausted, go on to the next participant for him or her to choose the next question they would like to see discussed, and then repeat the process. Of course, this all should be done on a voluntary basis. This continues until all the questions of interest to the participants are discussed on this particular questionnaire. Then we can go on to the next questionnaire and repeat the process, until all the questionnaires are covered. When you finish with this exercise, then hopefully you'll begin to understand the full extent of the Christian faith. Also these latter two methods are a possible means whereby you could train future Christian Discussion Leaders for adults, and even adolescents. .

AT THE END OF EACH CHAPTER YOU WILL FIND SPACE THAT IS PROVIDED FOR YOU IN TRYING TO ANSWER SOME OF THE QUESTIONS THAT YOU MIGHT BE REFLECTING UPON.

Chapter 1

CONVERSION TO CHRIST AND HOW TO COMMUNICATE CHRIST MORE EFFECTIVELY

The purpose of this questionnaire is to help people understand how they came to know Jesus Christ, and then how they can communicate Him to others, or in other words: Evangelism. Although it might be easy to communicate our faith with other Christian, it becomes much more difficult to share our faith with non-Christians, and this discussion guide hopefully will help you with this. A further purpose for this guide as a lead-off is that without effective faith communication, our efforts to deal with other Christian concerns become fruitless. After all, we might be the first Bible people will read as we try to imitate Christ. Two pastors found these questions most interesting and stimulating. Some of these questions might be pertinent to your life, others maybe not. Only consider those questions that are meaningful to you, which might take only one sitting, or more. But it might be helpful if these questions were reviewed by the participants a week before they're discussed. **Rom. 10:9, John 4:1-26, John 8:4-11, Rom 10:9-15, Etc.**

QUESTIONS

1. What is conversion, and what has been your experience in coming to Christ?

2. What is Sin, and how does it relate to you in coming to Christ?

3. If you felt you were called by God for a certain type of ministry, what 4 tests could you use to determine whether this is really a call from God or not? See Supp. 1 Below

4. What is the Basic Function of the Church?

5. How do you communicate Christ? In business, in your neighborhood, at home, Etc.?

6. What do you think of the Socratic method (listening and asking probing questions), at least in helping the listener recognize his or her need for a Savior, as a communication tool?

7. How many people have you saved (converted) or led to Christ in the past twelve months?

8. Should a Christian determine (judge) who is or is not a Christian when communicating his or her faith?

9. Should a Christian communicate his or her faith through mental persuasion, or through witnessing at an opportune moment what faith has done for him or her? Who really converts, the Christian or the Holy Spirit? Once you're saved, are you always saved?

10. What is your relationship to the Holy Spirit, and what is His relationship with you?

11. In your Church, assuming that you had the authority, would you try to set up an Evangelistic program if none existed? Why or why not?

12. What is Evangelism and does the word "Evangelism" have a bad connotation? Why or why not?

13. Should your church emphasize Evangelism or Christian Growth?

14. Should it be more important to try to get people into Heaven or to get Heaven into people?

15. In a pastor, should one look for leadership or shepherdship? By leadership I mean one who leads without looking back to see if he has lost any of his congregation. By shepherdship I mean one who follows his flock to take care that he does not lose any of his congregation.

16. Would the best approach in teaching the Gospels be by teaching them concurrently or as a whole rather than in teaching them separately as the Gospel of Matthew, Mark, Luke, and. John? Have you ever tried this approach?

17. Is setting up neighborhood Bible or Gospel study groups whereby you can invite your neighbours in to participate, a good tool to use in communicating Christ? Can and could you use it in your situation?

18. One person suggested that since we have two ears and one mouth, we should listen twice as much as we speak. Do you, agree?

19. Some Conservative people suggest that since God never changes, why should we change or the way we do things change. The problem here, as I we see it, is that if we want to grow, we have to accept changes. If we don't, we'll never grow. What do you think?

20. Should communicating Christ be more of a dialogue rather than a monologue to be most effective?

21. If a person rejects the Christian message, is he or she really rejecting Christ or the Christian messenger? .

22. Do you feel one should write out a Personal Mission Statement (What one feels God wants him or her to do in life to further the Kingdom of God) to improve his or her witnessing for Christ? See Supp. 2 below

23. In conclusion, how do you feel, either through Internet or otherwise, we can continually educate Christians on how to communicate Christ more effectively?

Supplement 1

BEING CALLED BY GOD THROUGH JESUS CHRIST
Excerpts from a book entitled "Dimensions of Decisions" by Newell J. Wert by
Corbin M. Wright

If you feel that you are being called by God for a certain type of ministry, you have to test these feelings, because you can never really trust your own feelings. They might be the result of some hidden experience you already had or from the Devil. Now there are 4 ways in which you can actually test these feelings to see if they really do come from God.

1) Is it Biblically sound? But you have to be careful how you use the Bible. Unfortunately there are many Christian who take the Bible out of context and try to prove a point by taking Scriptural passages out of the context of the true meaning of the particular section. You have to take the Bible as a whole to understand as to whether your call is Biblically sound or not. A second caution I would make here is that in many cases you will not get a direct answer to a specific decision you will have to make. You will only get general guidance from the Bible.

2) Look around and see what God is doing in the world. Is this ministry that you feel you're being called to do, something in line with what God is doing in the world? In other words, would you be helping God in His efforts to improve the world?.

3) What does your conscience say? Is this ministry that you feel you're being called to do, go against your conscience? But you have to be careful here also. The conscience can receive many messages: Some from God, some from your early childhood, not related to God, and some even from the Devil. So you have to be extra cautious about your conscience.

4) Is your call reasonable? God gave us the ability to use reason so it stands to reason that God would use this ability for us to determine whether this call is legitimate or not. For example, if you feel you received a call to go to Africa and you had a sick mother or invalid father at home with nobody to take care of them if you went flying off to Africa, would this call really come from God. In other words, before you accept the call, you also have to think of the after consequences of your decision. If

the call is legitimate and comes from God, I'm sure God will remove any barriers that would prevent you from accepting His call. But you do have to think of the after consequences if you accept the call, and wait for God to remove any barriers that would bar you from accepting His call.

Supplement 2

A Personal Mission Statement

Rick Warren in his book "The Purpose-Driven Life" suggests that a Personal Mission Statement to be most effective is one whereby you can discover your SHAPE. By this I mean, S stands for what Spiritual Gift you would like to use in your communication (see Eph 4:11-13, I Cor 12:4-10, and Rom 12:6-8). H stands for Heart, or what kind of passion you would have for this particular Spiritual Gift. This passion would also be provided by the Lord. A stands for what kind of Ability do you have which the Lord also gave you in using this Spiritual Gift (some have administrative skills, others have skills with their hands or numbers, others have musical or language skills, while others have people skills, etc). P stands for whether your Personality (extrovert or introvert) lends itself in your using this particular Spiritual Gift effectively. And E stands for what kind of Experience in other endeavours have you had in the past in using this Spiritual Gift. All of these thoughts on SHAPE, I believe, would help you in being a more effective communicator for our Lord.

EVANGELISM

**THIS PAGE SHOULD BE USED TO WRITE ANSWERS TO THOSE
QUESTIONS IN THIS CHAPTER IN WHICH YOU'RE INTERESTED.
IF NECESSARY, USE ADDITIONAL PAPER.**

Chapter 2

HOW TO COPE WITH SUFFERING

The reason for this discussion guide is for Christians to be able deal with the most basic question that most people have as to why they don't believe in Christianity, or even in God. **In other words, why does God allow so much Pain and Suffering in the world when He's so Powerful and Good? And with all this Pain and Suffering, what can we do about it? What are some of the procedures we can actually follow to relieve people from this Horrendous Experience?** What about Prayer, Bible Readings and Study, Christian Companionship, Forgiveness, and Praise? **Also how can one ever Grow in Understanding without Experiencing some sort of Suffering themselves?** Here again, some of these questions might be pertinent to your life, others maybe not. Only consider those questions that are meaningful to you, which might take only one sitting, or more. But it might be helpful if these questions were reviewed by the participants a week before they're discussed to see what is of interest to them. **Math 27:46, Math. 6:12, Jer. 31:34, I Thes 5:18. Etc..**

QUESTIONS

1. What causes Suffering? And if there is a loving and powerful God, why do so many Christians and good people have to suffer so much whereas others don´t? What about natural disasters?

2. If we knew all the reasons why people suffer, wouldn't we really be God?

3. What is Exorcism and do you believe in it?

4. In suffering, why are some people so sensitive, and others not, over the same event? Give examples.

5. Do you believe in Euthanasia or Mercy Killing?

6. Do you believe in Abortion where it can alleviate some of the suffering? Explain.

7. Without pain, can we really grow spiritually and mentally? Do we need at least some pain for this? A) As we grow, will the pain generally become less and less?. B) Without our own pain to some degree, and even in a different area of life, can we really help others?

8. In suffering or pain, why does forgiveness play such an important part in the situation? A) Do you have to forgive, if you don't condemn? B).Can you argue with someone without condemning him or her? C) Do you also have to forgive institutions or situations which you've condemned in your anger? D) What about forgiving God?

9. Why is forgetfulness of the bitterness so necessary in true forgiveness?. A) Can forgetfulness be accomplished by your thanking God for everything that happens to you? B) Can forgetfulness be accomplished by empathizing with the person who hurt you?

10. Why do people commit Suicide and what can one do to prevent someone from committing Suicide? One might find a possible answer in Supp.# 1 Below.

11. Is it all right to become angry at God? What happens then?

12. Does prayer really work? Give examples.. A) Is meditation really a form of prayer? See below.

So if there is a God, why doesn't He seem to answer prayer? This is a difficult question to answer, but it's probably due to the consequences of sin and spiritual warfare taking place around us, although in our prayers one can experience God being with us to comfort and heal us in any of the suffering we're encountering. The basic function of prayer, however, is to build a faith relationship between God and ourselves, and petitionary prayer is only a small part of this faith relationship. But with petitionary prayer being the crux of the problem as to whether prayer works or not, you can never scientifically prove that petitionary prayer really works, because there are so many interconnected variables to look at in God's scheme of things. Sometimes prayer seems to work, and sometimes it doesn't, but here you have to realize our loving God has a much broader perspective as to what is really needed for society's betterment, than we do while we're here on earth. And as I said above, you also have to take into account the consequences of sin, and spiritual warfare

13. How do you explain the contradiction in prayer, which are both Biblical, that you're supposed to pray for the healing of individuals (Luke 11:9-10), but at the same time you're to thank God for their illnesses (I Thes 5:18)?

14. Does Bible reading or the memorization of Biblical verses help? Give examples.

15. Faith helps when one is suffering, but what kind of Faith and how does one get this type of faith?

16. If you had enough Faith, would you be suffering? If you are saved, would you be healed?

17. Should one lie in order to prevent another from suffering? Are there other situations in which lying could be acceptable?

18. I know a Christian who has never suffered, despite having some experiences that we all seem to consider as being tragic? Could you explain this? Could you really define what suffering is and what its purpose might be if one suffers?

19. As Christians, some feel that we need to suffer to identify with Christ's suffering, whereas others feel that we shouldn't suffer, since Christ did the suffering for us? What do you think?

20. Do you feel excessive boredom or the creation of excessive boredom is a sin, and that this can create much suffering?

21. Do you feel that developing a general support group in your Church would help those who are suffering? One might call this a growth or support group.

22. Many Christians feel that Suffering comes from Man's Free Will, Creation's Limitations, and Unseen Spiritual Conflict . What do you think, and which do you think is the most predominant?

23. Comment on some of these answers in coping with suffering: A) Participating in Self-Improvement Programs, B) Practicing Positive-Thought Recitations, C) Imagining you´re one of your more Positive Thinking Acquaintances, D) Participating in a Support Group, E) Visiting a Psychologist or a Psychotherapist, F) Going to a Prayer Group, G) Doing things for others, H) Taking care of pets, I) Human-cloning, or organ or gene transplanting, j) Abortion, K) Euthanasia, L) Suicide.

24. How can we continually educate people on how to effectively deal with suffering or pain? Possibly by reading one of crippled-for-life Joni Eareckson's books.

If you want an even more Biblical study on suffering turn to "The Book of Job", or if you want a Christian-psychology approach turn to "A Road Less Traveled" by M.. Scott Peck M.D. Also if you want a more therapeutic approach in trying to help those who are suffering, you should try to set up some type of Support Group or Growth Group in your Church.

Supplement 1

How to Deal with Suicides

The following is a report that indicates how you might recognize suicidals, and how you might deal with them. But a warning: Suicide can be a very complex issue, and it might be better to have a professional deal with this issue if it comes up, but if this is very difficult to attain, this guide is a possible alternative to follow if you have no other solution to the problem.

Summary of Book "CHOOSING TO LIVE" by Dr. Thomas E. Ellis & Dr. Cory F.Newman

A suicidal person once said "It's like I want to be dead, but not forever:"

1) Suicide is an Ugly Word.—To help get rid of this stigma, you should think of suicide as a problem-solving situation. Basically there is no such thing as a rational suicide with the possible exception of Euthanasia.

2) Who are the Suicidals?—Basically there are two types. They are either extremely depressed, manifested in many ways and many times deeply hidden, (mostly with men), or they are extremely controlling (mostly with women). The extremely depressed are interested in death (life is too painful for them) whereas the extremely controlling just want attention and are afraid of abandonment. One way in dealing with the recognizable potential suicidals, if you can eliminate the stigma in talking about suicide, is to set up two columns (one headed "advantages of living" and the other headed "advantages of dying") on a piece of paper, and have the potential Suicidal list the various advantages as he or she sees it. If the advantages of dying outweigh the advantages of living, the counselor has to work with the potential suicidal on the advantages of living. Some of the risk factors that one should look for in assessing whether one is suicidal or not are 1) has he or she tried it before, 2) has suicide been part of the family's history, 3) is the person deeply depressed or extremely withdrawn, 4) is there excessive substance abuse or prolonged abuse of any kind, and 5) is there a specific plan in place to commit suicide.

3) Who are the Suicidals—Continued—They are usually the people with strong negative backgrounds, either genetically or environmentally. And to help those with this heritage, it's good to continue encouraging those with these suicide tendencies to continue listing reasons for living on a piece of paper.

4) Should Suicidals be Changed?—No, but their decision-making skills have to be greatly improved, which means they have to see both sides of an issue in order to make an intelligent decision. This means they also have to see the advantages of suicide with their various downsides in order to make an intelligent choice. This should all be done on paper as well so that the potential suicidals can see it all written down before them.

5) Handling a Suicidal Impulse Crisis.—One should try to delay the suicidal impulse crisis, so that the crisis would no longer be so urgent to complete. And to do this you could encourage the Suicidal to sleep it off, talk to a trusted friend about their situation, (This is why the Suicide Prevention hotline is so important), or call 911 or any other emergency telephone number. A longer delaying tactic could be to have them reflect in writing on any unfinished business they would want to accomplish before they die, and encourage them to pursue these goals. Then they should start to enjoy living again. And a third possibility would be for the Suicidals to begin nurturing themselves by keeping themselves well groomed, listening to soothing music, enjoying good food, appreciating beautiful scenes or looking after their pets. But this will take some initial will power.

6) Thinking and Feeling—You feel what you think, whether consciously or unconsciously, but your thoughts are not necessarily facts.

7) How to Change One's Thinking—To change one's negative suicidal feelings, one has to change one's thinking. There are several ways in which to do this. There is the functional approach (after the negative thought surfaces, ask yourself where is it getting me), the logical/empirical approach (after the negative thought surfaces, ask yourself where is the evidence for such a thought), and the questioning approach (after the negative thought surfaces, ask yourself are there other possibilities for such a happening). You can try all these approaches and see what works best for you. Everyone is different. But always do this in writing because it stays with you much longer, and persevere in your efforts because it's only successful if you keep on trying. And if none of these methods work, try the behaviour approach whereby do the opposite of what you're feeling, because eventually your behaviour will start to effect and change your thinking.

8) Coping with Suicidal Feelings—There are also ways to accommodate your feelings while you're in the process of adjusting your thinking. This can be done by obtaining support from empathizers, ventilating your feelings appropriately, engaging in constructive distractions, or participating in enjoyable recreational activities, and practicing various relaxation techniques (ie, meditation).

9) Learning to Solve Problems—Suicidals actually believe that death is the solution to all problems, but suicide is really the problem to end all solutions. So if you want to solve problems, you have to forget about death. And if you're underestimating your ability to solve problems, you should look at your past experience in recalling if you solved other people's problems as well as your own.. If you did, it suggests that you still have the capability in solving problems. But what are the ingredients that you need in order to solve problems efficiently. There are actually 6. They are 1) that you have to have the problem-solving mind-set, 2) that you have to have the ability to define the problem, 3) that you have to have the ability to generate alternative ideas to solve problems (brainstorming), 4) that you have to evaluate these ideas and decide on a course of action, 5) that you then have to take this action and test the results, and 6) that you have to realize that the results don't have to be perfect.

10) Other Skills to Improve your Life—There are some other approaches you can use to lessen suicidal tendencies. Some of these are 1) learning how to become more assertive, 2) improving your relationship-enhancement skills by making your presence known to others, being responsive to kind words and invitations, making a point of treating others with consideration and respect, and learning relationship skills through how you associate with your pets, and 3) involving yourself strongly in helping other people.

11) Developing a Philosophy of Life—But behind all these techniques, one has to discover a new, but meaningful philosophy of life for these potential suicidals, so

that they would CHOOSE TO LIVE a much more abundant life, as opposed to dying prematurely. Find out how Christianity might help in this regard.

Appendix—Guide for Concerned Friends

Signs to Look for 1) The person talks about suicide. 2) The person makes final plans. (gives away prized possessions) 3) The person's behavior pattern changes in disturbing ways. 4) The person behaves in ways that are self-injurious or stem to invite danger or harm. 5) The person has experienced significant losses in a short period of time. 6) The person suffers from a chronic illness. 7) The person has suffered extreme social humiliation. 8) The person abuses mind-altering substances and has access to firearms or other instruments of self-destruction. 9) The person has tried it before. 10) Suicide seems to run in the family.

In any of these situations, don't overreact or under-react, take the middle ground and dialogue with the suicidal to see what's really going on with him or her in a very calm, and non-judgmental way. But don't ever feel his or her feelings are your responsibility. They have to make the choice themselves whether they want to live or die.

Summary of the book by Corbin M. Wright

SUFFERING

**THIS PAGE SHOULD BE USED TO WRITE ANSWERS TO THOSE
QUESTIONS IN THIS CHAPTER IN WHICH YOU'RE INTERESTED.
IF NECESSARY, USE ADDITIONAL PAPER.**

_____

_____

_____

_____

_____

_____

_____

_____

_____

_____

_____

_____

_____

_____

_____

_____

_____

_____

_____

_____

_____

_____

Chapter 3

MUCH SUFFERING IS CAUSED
BY ECONOMIC FACTORS

One of the most prolific forms of Suffering one finds in the world today is that of ECONOMIC SUFFERING, either perceived or actual. And hopefully this discussion will lead in helping you find more contentment in your particular economic situation by indicating to you e.g. How to Look for a Job, or How to Become Financially Independent. Here again, only consider those questions that are pertinent to your life..And again, it might be helpful if these questions were reviewed by the participants a week before they're discussed to see what is of interest to them. **Math 6:24, Math 13:22, Eccl 5:10, Phil 4:19, Etc.**

QUESTIONS

1. Does increasing the supply of one's money help in alleviating suffering?

2. Is Gambling a Sin? What about the State Lottery, or Church Bingo?

3. If one has lost a job, or needs one that is more lucrative or meaningful, how does one go about looking for a job? What about the Haldane approach where you can develop direct contact with the Corporate decision-makers? See Supp # 1 And what about becoming an Entrepreneur? See Supp # 2 Would it help, if the church organized an Employment Support Group? See Supp # 3

4. Is or will there be enough work, with adequate remuneration, for all the people on this planet who are able to work now or in the future? If the answer is "No", what can be done about it? If the answer is "Yes", why is there so much unemployment around the world today?

5. What can one do about World Hunger or Health Care?

6. What can one do about Illegal Immigration which is caused by so much Economic Suffering in other countries?

7. How can you become Financially Independent? See Supp. # 4

8. If you have a strong faith, does this guarantee great material wealth, if it's your wish?

9. .Is Money or the Love of Money the Root of all Evil? If neither, What is?

10. What can one do about Poverty?

11. In a job, should you look for personal success such as in fame, money, power, or etc. or in social job significance? And whatever option you choose, how would you attain it?

12. What part should the Federal or Local Governments play in Economic Suffering? What is the best type of Economy, Capitalistic or Socialistic? See Supp. # 5 below.

13. What part should the United Nations or International Institutions play in Economic Suffering?

14) What part should Charities or Churches play in Economic Suffering?

Supplement 1

How to Look for a Job

A) Before doing anything, you have to determine what you really want to do in life job-wise. To do this, if you don't already know your life's ambition, you should take some psychological tests from a professional to see what your interests are and to see what your aptitude is; and then to put them both together to determine in what direction you want your life to go. After this, you can concern yourself with your resume or curriculum.

B) The Chronological Curriculum:

1. First and foremost you have to be able to write an effective resume or curriculum. Now there are two types of curriculums that you have to consider. One is the Chronological Curriculum while the other is the Functional Curriculum. But since the Chronological Curriculum is the one that is most used, I'm going to start in explaining how to most effectively write and use this one. 2. One of the most important items often left out of this type of curriculum is the objective or direction that you're trying to set-up for yourself. In other words you should have some idea as to what kind of position or job you're applying for and state this in a very bold fashion either at the top of the curriculum or in a covering letter. Otherwise your curriculum will probably be ignored. 3. Thirdly, your curriculum should be no longer than two pages, preferably one, and written on paper that highlights your skills. 4. Fourthly, your schooling and job experience should start with the most recent to the least recent. 5. Fifthly, your experiences whether schooling or working should start with those experiences that are most recent and most related to the position you're applying for. Also if you have university experience you normally don't have to put down your primary or secondary school experience. 6. And finally, if you know more than one language or have a specialized skill or interest that could relate to the position that you're applying for, put this in a most prominent place on your curriculum. After finishing this, your curriculum can be distributed as a result

of newspaper ads, Internet, or any other situation that might lead to a potential job that you might be interested in.

C) The Functional Curriculum:

1. The Functional Resume or Curriculum, however, is the one that is much less frequently used. The reason for this is that, although you normally would get a better job, you have a lot more to do to put this curriculum into operation. 2. To begin with you should write the story of your own life, but only the positive aspects of it. Then you should mention the talents that you used to make these life events so positive. After this you have to rank the five most important talents (1,2,3,4,5) that you used. 3. On the other end of the scale you have to determine the direction you want your life to take job wise based on your past experiences and education. Then you have to relate those 5 talents mentioned above to your job search by writing them in importance order under your goal, and giving two examples of each on how you used these talents in the past, but related to experiences that would help you in your job search. This then is your curriculum. Goal + Talents + 2 Examples after each talent. 4. After finishing the curriculum you do not send it out. You memorize it, not in the sense that you're memorizing it word for word, but in the sense that you should memorize the essential essence of the curriculum. Then practice the verbalization of it with trusted friends. 5. In the meanwhile you should start contacting by letter executive decision makers in your areas of interest of companies that you would like to work for, but not asking them for a job. Instead you would be asking them for an interview whereby they can give you some advice on what you could do with your talents, and you should mention to them in the letter that in a few days you will be contacting them by telephone to set up such a meeting. But remember; don't contact the personnel directors unless you want to work in that area, but the decision makers who can usually override their personnel directors. 6. At the interview, remember that with a Chronological Curriculum the interviewer controls the interview, but with your verbalizing the Functional Curriculum in front of the interviewer, the interviewee controls the interview. 7. Using this approach you can develop many important contacts because your initial interviewer can put you in contact with many people at the same executive level of companies similar to the one you're interested in, if he or she's impressed with your presentation. Also remember this: Many times when you're dealing with executive decision makers and they like your capabilities, they could create a job for you if none is currently available.

D) Suggestions on Interviews:

1. Always dress neatly and somewhat conservatively. 2. Never be a "yes" person. Always express your honest opinion, but in a way that shows respect for the other person's opinion. 3. Appear enthusiastic. 4. And always send a thank you note after each interview.

This information was attained from two executive employment agencies in New York.

Supplement 2

Entrepreneurship

An entrepreneur can be defined as someone who is in control of his or her own destiny and who makes things of economic consequence happen.

To be an entrepreneur you have to have a particular kind of mindset. That is, you have to have; 1) a strong desire, 2) perseverance, 3) initiative, 4) persuasive skills. 5) a winning attitude and 6) a bottom line mentality.

To begin with you should write down your concept as to what you economically want to do as precisely as you can in only one paragraph. But in doing this you have to watch out for the various traps that exist in developing a concept. They are; 1) it won't work, 2) you can't make any money on it, 3) there is no market for it, and 4) there can be unpredictable customer behaviour. But also remember this; that the customer has to pay at least 5 times the direct cost of a product.

Now there are three types of Business entries that you should consider. They are; 1) starting from scratch whereby you should be prepared to take 5 to 8 years to start a business, 2) buying an existing business whereby the risks are less by saving time (1 year) for the business to be operational, buying cheaper assets, and by assuming cheaper financing, and/or 3) in buying a franchise whereby the risk would only be about 30%. Also you could be an Entrepreneur within a company as well.

The ideal business actually should have; 1) no investment, 2) an identifiable market, 3) a low cost supply, 4) minimum government regulations, 5) good price-cost ratio, 6) frequent buyers, 7) favourable tax treatment, 8) a good distributing system, 9) news value, 10) technical fashion obsolescence, 11) perishability and, 12) weather proofness.

Three types of business plans should be written once your concept of a business starts to materialize. They are; 1) The Feasibility Plan, 2) The Operational Plan and, 3) The Financial Plan. Financing for the business could be accomplished by; 1) cash from customers, 2) sub-contracting, 3) your own money, 4) borrowing (from as few as possible) or 5) by leasing.

The Management team, if you decide to assemble one, should include; 1) the creator, 2) the driving force, 3) the marketer (the marketing strategy should be to find the competitive edge either in quality, price, or service) and, 4) a financial expert. Then you should give each of them part of the rock and teach them to listen to others.

This knowledge came from a film entitled "Winning Entrepreneur Style" by the University of Southern California.

An Entrepreneur, who became a millionaire, suggested on television that the key to his success came from reading just one book: And that was the Book of Proverbs from the Bible.

Supplement 3

An Employment Support Group

This group could meet once a week, more importantly in a church setting because of its Spiritual dimensions, for about an hour a week. The members should then introduce themselves and then give a summary of what type of job they might be looking for. Then someone during the middle of the session, who is somewhat knowledgeable about the subject, could give a short talk on a particular aspect of the job search, such as the search plan, networking, the resume, etc. And finally at the end of the session each member could explain what they plan to do in their job search for the coming week.

Then during the week the leader of the group could sit down with one member of the group each week to go over individually with what that member plans to do with his or her resume in his or her job search. Here the leader could discuss with this member their work habits, and how the time of their unemployment was affecting them and their families.

Many times their efforts might not end up with the type of job they were looking for, but most likely they will find some kind of a job in order to at least pay some of their bills. But oftentimes their efforts could send them onto much more successful careers in spite of or perhaps because of their loss of their previous job.

One of the problems that one might find here is that once a member might find a job, the member might feel that all his or her problems would be over. Oftentimes, however, the leader would also discover that their were some serious marital conflicts, problems with children, or difficulties with other interpersonal relationships that affected their job security. Here you might suggest some other types of professional help.

Supplement 4

How to Become Financially
Independent

1. First of all you don't have to have a lot of money to be financially independent. You only have to have enough. The question then becomes, what is really enough? The next question you have to ask yourself if you're working is "Am I earning a living" or "Am I earning a dying"?

2. To begin with, you have to take stock of what you now possess. That is, you have to prepare a balance sheet of your personal possessions. In other words you should determine your assets (what you own) and your liabilities (what you owe) and then subtract your liabilities from your assets to figure out what your net worth is. In this way you might find out that you're richer than you thought, poorer than you thought or just about where you thought you were. In fact one person found out when he did this that he really was a millionaire and didn't have to worry about being financially

independent anymore. But in any case it's important to know where you stand at this point in time.

3. As an aside here, I have to say we don't prepare budgets. We found that budgets are very much like diets and they usually don't work.

4. The second step you should take is to determine how much money you're really making on an hourly basis at your present job, or how much you're looking for hourly, if you are out of work. Now in determining this, you should not only figure in the hours and money that you receive while you're on the job, but also any time and deduction in expenses that have accrued to you that are really work related (travel to and from work, work related illnesses, costuming, decompression time and expenses related to work, etc.). In fact, one employee found that he was making a minus income if he stayed at his current job any longer.

5. The third step that you should take is to start keeping track of every cent that comes into and goes out of your life and to categorize each cent according to your judgment as to what categories or subcategories are essential in determining where your money is actually going and coming from. Then at the end of each month you should total all the categories or subcategories. After this you should subtract the expenses from the income. Then you can add or subtract the result depending upon whether there's a gain or loss for the month to a beginning cash balance. The result should equal the actual closing cash balance for the month plus or minus a human error in calculations. A gain for the month would be a savings.

6. Next you have to start by defining what money really is. Most would define money as a medium of exchange, but I would like to offer another definition. Money is what you trade your life energy for. And in looking at this definition you have to match the life energy that you're using with the totals in each of the categories or subcategories that you've listed to record your money spent. To do this you should use the formula; Dollars Spent / Real Hourly Wage = Hours of Life Energy Used.

7. The next step is to determine your goal or goals that you might have for the rest of your life. And in order to do this you might have to ask yourself a number of important questions. For example; 1) What did you want to be when you grew up? 2) What have you always wanted to do that you haven't done yet? 3) What have you done in your life that you're really proud of? 4) If you knew you were going to die in a year, how would you spend that year? 5) What brings you the most fulfillment—and how is that related to money? or 6) If you didn't have to work for a living, what would you do with your time?

8. Now once you've determined what your goal or goals are, you should match this purpose with the totals in each of the categories or subcategories to see if a particular expense is really in alignment with your purpose or not. If not, you might ask yourself how might that expense be adjusted accordingly. In doing this though you should also

be aware as to whether your purpose is in alignment with what's good for the planet as well.

9. Now here I doubly want to emphasize, and historical evidence seems to back me up, that unless your basic priority is the welfare of the planet, you will normally not be financially independent.

10. Next draw a wall chart indicating the trend upward or downward that your income and expenses are taking over a certain period of time. Use the vertical side of the graph to represent the money and the horizontal side to represent the movement of time. Also use different colored lines to distinguish between the income and expenses on the graph. Notice the trends. Within three months your expenses should decrease by 20%. Unusual expenses could be prorated or balance each other out. And eventually this wall chart should be made public for mutual encouragement.

11. Tips on how to start being frugal: 1) Stop trying to impress other people. 2) Don't go shopping unless you really need something. 3) Avoid using credit cards as much as possible. 4) Do it yourself. 5) Look for bargain quality. 6) Use your possessions efficiently. 7) Watch out for unnecessary interest payments and financial charges. 8) Check out your transportation costs. 9) It would be helpful if job and home were close together. 10) Go to a four day ten hour workweek. 11) Comparison shop for good medical services. 12) Reduce Stress. 13) Rent out unused space in your home. 14) Explore living in a commune where people have similar life-styles. 15) Live in a mobile or motor home. 16) Share your possessions. 17) Share your chores. 18) Vacation near home. 19) Have potlucks rather than dinner parties. 20) Develop inexpensive hobbies , 21) Do you need as much insurance as you're carrying and 22) Continue to use your imagination.

12. Now you should really start to redefine work as something you actually love to do rather than something you have to be paid for. In this way you can maximize your income while minimizing your time in acquiring it, so that you can value your life energy more effectively until you reach your goal or goals. In other words, you could work for pay for a limited period of time just to earn enough income to support yourself in the work that you really love to do.

13. With your new definition of work and your new scheme in how you should spend money, you should start your savings. I would say here that you might need a cushion of at least 6 months in savings with some interest being paid, for emergencies. After this, you should call your savings "Capital" which is the money you should put into long-term investments for making money.

14. Now these long-term investments should be as close to the following criteria as possible: 1) Your capital must produce income, 2) Your capital must be absolutely safe, 3) Your capital must be a totally liquid investment, 4) Your capital must not be diminished at the time of investment by unnecessary commissions, 5) Your income must be absolutely safe, 6) Your income must not fluctuate so that it would be the same

each month, 7) Your income should be payable to you in cash at regular intervals, 8) Your income must not be diminished by unnecessary charges, and 9) Your investment must require no maintenance charges of any kind. In the U.S. at the moment only one category of investment fits into this criteria and that is "Long-term U.S. Treasury and U.S. Government Agency Bonds".

15. And finally, along with your working income and expenses, with a third different coloured line you can record your steadily rising gains from your long-term investments on the wall chart as well. When this line eventually crosses over the expense line (called the crossover point), you can then consider yourself financially independent because your needed income is basically acquired through money, rather than through your individual work effort. I know that there is one 4 member family that discovered by using this approach that they could live on $300.00 a month comfortably.

This summarizes a book entitled "Your Money or Your Life" by Joe Domínguez and Vicky Robin

Supplement 5

PURE SOCIALISM DOES NOT WORK

To many people socialism sounds like a dream and in theory one might think of it as a utopia. But we have to be very careful about this because in the real world, pure socialism really doesn't work. In fact, they tried it in one country in Africa peacefully many years ago, and it turned out to be the poorest country in the world at that time. Capitalism has its problems too, because it always has its winners and losers, and how do you deal with the losers? But in socialism, in the long run, it only has losers. Why is this?

Because selfishness, or to put it more politely, self-interest is inborn in every individual, and governments can't change this, even though Socialism tries. In other words, in Socialism you don't have the incentive or motivational factor to better yourself materially that Capitalism has, and therefore you would tend not to work as hard or as creatively to achieve greater progress for yourself and eventually for society. What you gain for yourself would also be a gain for society. Governments can only use this self-interest factor to their advantage to create a better society. And therefore, I believe that Capitalism is the most effective system in doing this.

As I said above, there will be losers in this system as well, but here is where some type of socialism has to be used. So, in a sense, a balanced economy would really be the best where capitalism would be the prime motivating factor with socialism complementing it by guaranteeing that everyone would at least get all the necessities of life (food, health, water and shelter).. One should understand here though, that even if most countries believe in equality, Capitalistic countries believe that equality means having equal opportunities for achievement, whereas in Socialistic countries equality means having an equality in income. But one has to be careful here because the best way that the poor can actually be helped is that if they try to help themselves by getting the best education that they can possibly get so that they can compete in a thriving economy. Otherwise they will tend to drift into a laziness, that probably would become a generational habit, that would not help them grow into maturity. Therefore one has to realize that there will never be an economy where you will have an earthly equality, but capitalism, if it's practiced right, seems to be the best way in which you have the opportunity to try to accomplish this..

Corbin M. Wright corbinw@hotmail.com

ECONOMIC SUFFERING

THIS PAGE SHOULD BE USED TO WRITE ANSWERS TO THOSE QUESTIONS IN THIS CHAPTER IN WHICH YOU'RE INTERESTED. IF NECESSARY, USE ADDITIONAL PAPER.

Chapter 4

MUCH SUFFERING IS CAUSED BY POLITICAL FACTORS

Society is in a mess and if you want to engage in a discussion on **Political Suffering and how to deal with it, reflect upon and attempt to discuss the following questions. Someone once said that if you're not part of the Solution, you're really part of the problem. And these questions hopefully will teach you to devise ways in which Christians could influence their Political leaders to pursue policies that could influence World leaders to lessen the Political Sufferings of their people, as well as to influence their Political leaders to protect and improve the Political liberties they already have. In fact, your class could develop into a Political Lobbying Group on Christian issues.** Some of these questions might be pertinent to your life, others maybe not. Only consider those questions that are meaningful to you, which could take a number of sessions. But it might be helpful if these questions were reviewed by the participants a week before they're discussed to see what is of interest to them. **Duet 16:18-20, Mt. 17:24-27, Lk 20:20-26, Rom 13 1-7, I Tim 2:2, Etc.**

QUESTIONS

1. Do you feel Christians should be able to discuss any Political Issue in Church and how they should get involved in the Political Process? Why or Why not?

2. One of the most effective ways for Christians to be effectively involved in Political Activity is through individual or group lobbying efforts over an issue. What do you think? (See below on how this might work)

HOW DOES LOBBYING FOR AN ISSUE WORK

Group action would actually be more effective than individual action, although individuals can engage in lobbying activity as well, if group endeavours are not available. This action, group or individual, which could be taken in democracies as well as with international organizations, should be taken up as follows. 1) An intense study of the issue should be undertaken. 2) Then, you should decide how you want that issue changed, or if it should be. 3) If you want it changed, you should then find out which authorities you should contact to effect such a change. 4) Then, you should contact these authorities. 5) If the authorities don't respond to your satisfaction, contact them again (don't give up). 6) If the authorities continue to be unresponsive, contact them

again, but with a threat (use your imagination) that you feel might be injurious to their emotional well-being. But always with an exit strategy that these authorities could use. 7) If these authorities still remain unresponsive, follow through on the threat, and keep in mind other threats that could also be used against these authorities, if they're still unresponsive. And then, 8) Continue with steps 6 & 7, if you're still unsatisfied with the result of your efforts. I tried this approach and found that it works. In other words, if you're not part of the solution, you're really part of the problem.

3. What are some of the Political Domestic Issues that you'd like to deal with, and how would you like to deal with them? (e.g. The Economy, Drugs, Health Care. Crime, Homosexuality, Abortion, Pornography, Gun Control, Slavery, Etc.)

4 Do you believe in the Legalization of Marijuana? Of any Drug? Why or Why not?

5. Do you believe in Capital Punishment? Why or Why not? When, if?

6. Do you believe in better Gun Control? Why or Why not?

7. What are some of the Political Foreign Issues that you'd like to deal with, and how would you like to deal with them? (e.g. Terrorism, Israeli Conflict, War, Nuclear Dangers, Bacterial Dangers, Narcotics, Environmental Threats, World Hunger, Overpopulation, Slavery, Etc). See Supplements 2 & 3 below.

8. How would you prevent war?

9. How would you like to deal with the United Nations?

10. Politically, is it better to be Conservative, Moderate or Liberal? Why? See Supp # 1 Below.

11. Would it be best to have a Secular Government or a Religious Government? Why? See Supp # 4 below

12. Do you feel that if you're not part of the solution, you really part of the problem?

13. Many of the problems in the world today are caused by Hate. Now what can one do about all this Hate?

14. The struggle for Power is another big conflict that exists in the world today. Now what can one do to alleviate the need that so many people have to achieve this Power?

TO DEAL WITH THIS ISSUE OF HATE OR POWER ONE COULD DO THIS THOUGH VERBAL DIALOGUE OR NEGOTIATING. THE FOLLOWING IS A PROCEDURE FOR DOING THIS.

The Best Approach in Negotiating

   1. Participants are problem-solvers, not adversaries nor friends.

   2. The goal is a wise outcome reached efficiently and amicably.

   3. Separate the people from the problem.

   4. Be soft on the people, but hard on the problem.

   5. Proceed independent of trust.

   6. Focus on Interests, not positions.

   7. Explore Interests.

   8. Avoid having a bottom line.

   9. Invent options for mutual gain.

   10. Develop multiple options to choose from; decide later.

   11. Insist on objective material.

   12. Try to reach a result based on standards independent of will.

   13. Reason and be open to reason. Yield to principle, and not to pressure.

THIS BIBLE CLASS COULD REALLY TURN INTO A LOBBYING GROUP ON SOME OF THE CHRISTIAN ISSUES , IF IT WANTS. ALSO BE SURE GOD IS PRESENT WHENEVER YOU DISCUSS POLITICS BECAUSE POLITICS CAN BE SUCH A DIVISIVE ISSUE.

Supplement # 1

A CONSERVATIVE, MODERATE, OR LIBERAL

A Conservative recently said " Why can't we disagree with each other, and not invoke the emotion of hate toward each other as we discuss our different points of view". The problem, I believe, is in the use of the word "Conservative". After all, what does the word "Conservative" actually mean. It means "No Change". It actually means that we really live in a Perfect World, so why change anything. Conservatism itself becomes in effect a fighting word.

It's somewhat like the word "Liberalism". Liberalism in effect means that we should change everything. Liberalism too is a fighting word, and that's why so many people today try to avoid describing themselves as Liberals, even if they want to see many changes taking place in society.

I tend to be a Moderate with some Conservative ideas and some Liberal ideas, and I think this is the best position to be in, because then you tend to be open to any good Conservative ideas or any good Liberal ideas that you might come across In other words, you have many more options to choose from. So I think that in effect we all should really become Moderates. What do you think?

Corbin M. Wright

Supplement 2

Biblical Aspects of the Middle East Crisis

A POLITICAL CONCERN THAT HAS VERY IMPORTANT INTERNATIONAL RAMIFICATIONS.

In Genesis 13:15 God tells Abraham "All the land that you see I will give you and your offspring, Forever". God never considered Ishmael (the founder of the Arabs) part of his offspring, because Ishmael came from Sarah's handmaiden, not his wife. In Genesis 17:8 it states "The whole land of Canaan, where you are now an alien, I will give as an everlasting possession to you and your descendents after you, and I will be their God". In Genesis 17:21 it states "But my covenant I will establish with Isaac, whom Sarah will bear to you this time next year." Jacob, Isaac's youngest son, who stole the birthright from Esau, Isaac's eldest son, struggled with God and was thereafter called Israel (He struggled with God) Genesis 35:10. And after the Jews were led to Egypt to live, but eventually held in bondage, God spoke to Moses and said in Exodus 3:17 "And I have promised to bring you out of your misery in Egypt into the land of the Canaanites". And when Joshua took over from Moses the leadership responsibilities, God spoke to Joshua and said in Joshua 3:10 "This is how you will know that the living God is among you, and that He will certainly drive out before you the Canaanites—". But you notice, even in Scripture, the Israelites were never constantly remaining on the land God gave them. This is because that possession of the land came with a condition-Obedience to God. (Duet 4:1-2 and Duet 30:1-5).

And today, even though they have had their land for more than 50 years, it was founded on a secular, but cultural basis, and continues to be such with very little spirituality contained therein, so they continue to struggle for their land, because of economic jealousies. Or to put it another way, they continue to struggle with God.

Now the permanent restoration of Israel is not specifically mentioned in Scripture, but Jerusalem (the most important city in Israel) is mentioned as being permanently restored. But this, is in reality the New Jerusalem (Revelation 21) coming out of heaven and this would be the true City of Peace, which the name Jerusalem actually means. For Christians the restoration of the Promised Land now refers to the Kingdom of God (a Spiritual Realm), which comes only through Jesus Christ as stated in Galatians 3:29 "If you belong to Christ, then you are Abraham's seed, and heirs according to the Promise". This promise is the Promised Land, and therefore, for a Christian, the Promised Land is really the Kingdom of God in the hearts of the Believers, regardless of where they lived.

With this in mind, we should then recognize that Israel is only a Sovereign State, just like any other Sovereign State. Therefore, the negotiations are really taking place between a Sovereign State (Israel) and a potentially Sovereign People (the Palestines) and the negotiations should take place on an interest-interest basis (win-win situation), but unfortunately these negotiations are intermingled with religious dogma which do not lend themselves to a win-win situation because of the inflexibility of much of the dogma. Thus the problems between Israel and the Palestines which have to be resolved within this mixture are the current violence, the security for Israel, the Israeli settlements, the 2 state issue, the refugee problem, the Jerusalem situation, and the reconstruction of the Palestinian areas. But in order to do this, the religious dogma has to be toned down to make these negotiations much more of a win-win situation. But the Jerusalem situation could be resolved by declaring Jerusalem an International City honouring both the Jews, Christians, and Muslims because Jerusalem has played a very important part in the history of each of these religions.

Supplement 3

Weapons of Mass Destruction

Trying to control the proliferation of weapons of mass destruction is probably the most important issue facing the world's population today. It's certainly the most dangerous, because more and more countries are trying to develop these weapons. Now I'm talking more about the nuclear threat, rather than the bacterial and chemical threats, although these are just as dangerous and have to be controlled as well. The countries that we know that have these nuclear weapons at present are the USA, the United Kingdom, France, Russia, China, India, Pakistan, probably Israel, possibly South Africa, and definitely North Korea. Many also believe that Iran is trying to get a nuclear weapon, although they claim they're only trying to attain nuclear energy for peaceful purposes. But right now the world is more concerned about North Korea which does have nuclear weapons, but has an unpredictable and untrustworthy dictator, and Iran, even though they actually don't have nuclear weapons. They are worried about Iran because most countries in the world seem to feel that Iran desires them and could use them because they do possess a very radical and unpredictable religious belief that could justify their use. But behind all this is the fear that terrorists who have no national identity or allegiance might get their hands on these very dangerous weapons. And this is the real danger. Countries can be somewhat controlled, but individuals can be quite elusive. And the more countries that have this nuclear weaponry, the more dangerous it is that this nuclear weaponry could fall into the hands of these terrorists.

While many are trying to negotiate with North Korea so that they would get rid of its nuclear arsenal, and are also trying to prevent Iran from attaining nuclear weapons, there is really a contradiction here. While the many are trying to do this, they never talk about getting rid of their own nuclear weaponry. After all, the many feel that we're the good guys, and they're the bad. But how do North Korea and Iran really feel about this? Maybe they feel that they're the good guys, and we're the bad. It really tends to be a very subjective issue. But we're the stronger of the two groups who possess nuclear weapons, so we can actually exert much more pressure upon the smaller of the groups to get rid of them. This doesn't make it right, however. The problem, as I see it, is one of sovereignty. As long as you have sovereignty (individual countries) in the world., you're going to have each country trying to attain much more power at the expense of the others, and one of the most visible ways to demonstrate this power is through the military with a nuclear arsenal being the most powerful indication of this. This is also called competition which we're all trying to promote, but this is the most dangerous form of competition that the world can participate in.

The answer is actually in augmenting The Global Economy. By doing this, you're forcing countries to lessen their fear of losing their political sovereignty in order to develop a better life-style for their people which the Global Economy promises to establish worldwide. This in turn would create much more of a demand for cooperation among all the nations. And part of this cooperation will concern itself with their security. And this will also result in more of a demand for greater democratization and secularism in their governments so that the people will have much more of a say in how this type of economy should work.. Therefore, you'll find that dictators will have less of a hold on their people, and that a specific religion controlling a country will be a thing of the past. Concerning this latter case, a country in the future should never be Islamic, Jewish, or Christian, but only Secular with a tolerance for all religions and how they practice it as long as it's not forced upon the others. Thus, the growth of the Global Economy will tend to create peaceful cooperation, including security operations, among all the nations. Of course, you'll always have individuals who will try to attain nuclear weaponry for destructive purposes, but you'll also have much more protection for the nuclear facilities in these countries when you have them cooperating with each other.

Supplement 4

A Secular or Religious Government
What Do You Want?

If you're setting up a country, who would you like to govern it? Would you like a secular country or one basically controlled by a particular religion? By secular I mean one who allows all religions freedom to practice their own faith without infringing upon the rights of others to practice theirs, but at the same time controlling or governing the earthly part of their lives.

To begin with one has to examine the various countries around the world and to see how they're governed. Most countries are secular in nature, but there are a number of countries controlled or at least greatly influenced by a particular religion. Those countries controlled or greatly influenced by a religion are mostly Islamic. They are Iran, Syria, Iraq, Afghanistan, Indonesia, Pakistan, Palestine and a number of others. And of course there is always Israel which is controlled by the Jews. But in the past you also had the Roman Catholic Church controlling many countries. Today they're still trying, but their influence has been greatly diminished. I might add here that in some of these Islamic countries, there still seems to be a great struggle going on between secularism and Islam as to who should really govern.

Now the biggest conflict in the world today is between countries governed or greatly influenced by a particular religion. They are basically the Islamic States and the Jewish state, Israel. Now as an aside, what has caused this conflict? I believe it basically started in 1917 when Great Britain, which controlled the area at the time, agreed to set up the State of Israel right on top of some Islamic or Palestinian lands. This was finalized right after the Second World War. This meant that many of the Palestines had to move from their homeland to another place. Of course this has angered many of the Islamic peoples and this conflict has been going on ever since. Now why did Britain's western allies go along with this? Well there were several reasons for this. One reason is that the victorious allies in the Second World War felt very guilty about the Holocaust which they failed to prevent during the war, so they felt that they had to give the Jews a homeland where they could feel safe. After all the Jews have always been persecuted throughout the centuries for one reason or another, and this could provide a safe haven for them. But one might ask, why this particular land? That is, because the Jews believe that this is the land that God originally gave them, and the Christians, which make up most of the victorious allies, knew their faith originated from here, and therefore found a common bondage with the Jews in establishing a new homeland in this particular locality. Of course, today from a Christian perspective, we feel that the new homeland or Kingdom of God should really be found in a person's heart, regardless of where they lived.

Now getting back to the main theme of this article, I believe that the prime problem concerning this is that those countries that are more secular seem to be more successful in providing their people with a better standard of living. Why is this? I believe it is because if a country is controlled by a particular religion or is greatly influenced by one, it tends to control freedom of thought to a great extent. And when a country tends to control freedom of thought, it tends to limit access to new ideas on how to improve upon one's life. This is what happened in the past when the Roman Catholic Church controlled so many countries. Those countries that were controlled by the Roman Catholic Church did not progress as fast as those countries which basically had a secular form of government. For example, look at the difference between Latin America and the United States. Now today the same thing probably could happen to those countries that are insisting that they become Islamic, or are insisting that they be guided by any other particular religion. This doesn't mean that countries shouldn't be influenced by intangible Spiritual values, but these values should not be accompanied by tangible ceremonial observances instituted by the State. This same reasoning in controlling freedom of thought can be applied to those countries that tend to be authoritarian as well.

POLITICAL SUFFERING

THIS PAGE SHOULD BE USED TO WRITE ANSWERS TO THOSE QUESTIONS IN THIS CHAPTER IN WHICH YOU'RE INTERESTED. IF NECESSARY, USE ADDITIONAL PAPER.

Chapter 5

HOW TO DEAL WITH CHRISTIAN UNITY

The purpose of this discussion guide is to see how we might attain **Christian Unity which Jesus Christ so urgently demands. John 17:20-23. This guide will lead to a discussion on some of the things that really divide Christians as well as to a better dialogical understanding of those divisions that hopefully will unite Christians into a much more cooperative fellowship. This guide will also try to bring to light some of the ways that one might deal with what many Christians call the Christian Sects.** Here again, some of these questions might be pertinent to your life, others maybe not. Only consider those questions that are meaningful to you, which might take only one sitting, or more. But it might be helpful if these questions were reviewed by the participants a week before they're discussed to see what is of interest to them. **Acts 1:15, Acts 4:32, I Cor 12:13, Etc.**

Questions

1. What do you think causes Christian Divisions?

    A) Is denominationalism (Christian dividing) a sin?

2. What is Christian Ecumenism and how do you feel about it?

    A) Do you believe for Christians to have complete spiritual unity, you need some sort of Church Organizational Unity? If so, what do you think would be the most difficult issue to deal with?

3. How do you think we should proceed in our controversies over the Lord's Supper or Holy Communion?

    A) How would you interpret the Lord's Supper?
    B) Do you believe that in interpreting the Lord's Supper, we're really using different words to express the same thing, which to a certain extent, will always remain an earthly mystery?
    C) Who do you believe should take Holy Communion? How often? And how important is the use of both elements (bread and wine) in Holy Communion?
    D) How essential is the Lord's Supper, Holy Communion or the Mass to Salvation?

4. How do you think we should proceed in controversies over Baptism?

A) How would you interpret Baptism? Should it be by Sprinkling or Immersion?

B) Should Baptism be only for those who are capable of belief, for believers and infants of same, or not necessarily be an outward ceremonial act? Is it necessary for Salvation?

C) How many Baptisms can you have, and is "Baptism of the Holy Spirit", where speaking in tongues is an essential manifestation, just another Baptism?

5. What is a sacrament, and how many activities do you recognize as such? Is this issue an important component in any ecumenical dialogue or for Salvation?

6. How does Free Will and Predestination fit into your over-all belief system?

7. What does it mean to be in the ordained ministry?

A) Who do you believe can perform Priestly functions (Baptism, Holy Communion, etc.)?
B) Do you feel that the ordination of Christians could eventually disappear because of its dividing Christians into two distinct classes?

8. How do you feel we should proceed in our controversies over the organizational structure of the various churches, if we're looking for organizational unity?

A) Could you eventually accept the Pope as the head of the entire Christian Church?
B) Do you believe that a United Organizational Church should be strongly controlled with limited diversity or loosely controlled with a wide variety of diversity?

9. Do you feel that the theory of Evolution can to some degree be compatible with God´s Creation Doctrine? To what extent? Why or why not?

A) Is creation still taking place?

10. Do you believe that the Bible literally describes the end of time? Give some examples. What might be some other interpretations of these examples?

11. Is the debate among Christians over the beginnings and the future of life really that important; and should not our concentration be more on the present and how we can serve God now?

12. Do you believe that the Bible is the Word of God or contains the Word of God? Martin Luther once compared the Bible to a baby carriage with the baby inside. There can be errors in the carriage, but not with the baby inside. Does the Word of God go beyond what's included in the Bible?

A) What is your interpretative approach to Scripture? Do you believe that the Bible is infallible according to each word that is written, or the message it contains?

B) What part does tradition play in your interpretation of Scripture?

C) What part does experience play in your interpretation of Scripture?

13. Do the Christian Conservatives (literalists) and Christian liberals (contextualists) need each other for the church to flourish? (see below)

Conservative Emphasis	Liberal Emphasis
1) Scripture is authoritative.	1) The Gospel Must engage contemporary Culture.
2) Creeds and Confessions are valuable and Vibrant Expression of Faith.	2) Christians must invite change in the Non-Essentials.
3) The Gospel changes lives.	3) The Gospel is a Force for social change.
4) Personal Piety is a response to God's Grace without being legalistic.	4) The Gifts of all Christians Must be Claimed by the Church.
5) Stewardship is a Joyous Responsibility.	5) Christians must be Ecumenical in Dialogue.

14. What part does tradition play in your Belief System?

15. Do you think Priests should have the right to marry?

16. Could you accept a Pastor who is divorced and remarried? If so, under what circumstances? Due to the trend in increased divorces within society, do you feel an answer might be long-term comprehensive pre-marital counselling sessions? If not, how do you feel we should deal with so many divorces?

17. How do you think we should proceed to dialogue with a Church that emphasizes Mariology and the Saints?

A) What is a Saint according to the Bible?

18. How does Sanctification (making someone Holy or Good) and Justification by Faith rank in order of priority in your belief system?

19. Do you think organizational unity should be a major goal in order to achieve Spiritual unity within the Christian Church? What are the advantages or disadvantages of Christian organizational divisions?

20. What role do you feel women should have in a church organizational structure?

21. How do you think the Church should handle the issue of Homosexuality? And if you feel Homosexuals are born as such, how would this effect your answer to this question?

22. How do you feel the Church should handle the issue of Abortion? Does the Bible condemn Abortion? Where?

23. How should the Church deal with Living Together or Sex before Marriage in Her teachings?

24. How do you think we should proceed with those Churches that many Christians feel are actually Christian Sects (Christians Scientists, Jehovah Witnesses, Mormons, etc.) that deny the Trinity (one in three persons and three in one person) as we understand it?

    A) Are there any other factors that determine whether a Christian Church is really a Christian Sect?

25. How do you feel we should proceed with an ecumenical dialogue with the Christian Scientists?

26. How do you feel we should proceed with a more active dialogue with the Jehovah Witnesses, especially when their belief dictates that Jesus, The Word, and God are completely separate beings, but in the Jehovah Witness's own Scripture it states in John 1:1 "In the beginning the Word was, and the Word was with God"? As I understand it from my interpretation of their Scripture it seems to indicate that Jesus and God are one, but at the same time two separate beings as well, which contradicts the basic Jehovah Witness's doctrine. What do you think about this and other Jehovah Witness' Doctrine?

27. How do you feel we should proceed with a more active dialogue with the Mormons, especially when you realize that in the *Book of Abraham in the Pearl of Great Price*, one of the three books along with the Bible that has equal authoritative status, you find that God told Abraham to lie, which suggests that, if this were true, God would be going against His very own nature? In the Bible, it only states that Abraham lied without God being involved at all (Gen 12:12-13). How do you deal with this latter concern and any of the other Doctrines that the Mormons believe in?

28. Which Christian Sect would be most difficult to deal with?

29. What can we learn from the Christian Sects? What do you think they can learn from us?

30. Would a more effective way to create a more active dialogue with the Sects be to invite members of the Sects to a discussion group such as this, or a Bible study group?

31. Can you disagree with someone and still respect his or her opinion considering the fact that you probably are speaking from two different backgrounds?

32. What' would your reaction be if someone said to you "Are you born again?"?

    A) How do you look upon Salvation?

33. How might you help a Church grow?

34. How else might you enhance unity among the Christian Churches?

I strongly feel that the future trend in churches will be churches that are Christian non-denominational. What do you think?

CHURISTIAN UNITY

THIS PAGE SHOULD BE USED TO WRITE ANSWERS TO THOSE QUESTIONS IN THIS CHAPTER IN WHICH YOU'RE INTERESTED. IF NECESSARY, USE ADDITIONAL PAPER.

_____

_____

_____

_____

_____

_____

_____

_____

_____

_____

_____

_____

_____

_____

_____

_____

_____

_____

_____

_____

_____

_____

_____

_____

_____

_____

_____

_____

_____

Chapter 6

WOMAN'S ROLE IN CHURCH AND SOCIETY AND "MARRIAGE"

The purpose of this discussion is to determine what truly is the role that women should play in the Church and Society.. Women are oftentimes placed in secondary positions in the Church's and Society's organizational structure, so is the Church and Society actually being hurt by all of this? What does the Bible say? **After all, what makes this discussion so important is that at least half the world's population would be effected by this issue, and it would be nice for them to know where they should stand Biblically in this scheme of things.** This discussion would hopefully clarify this issue and make our attitudes more in tune with the Bible **Also one finds here questions on Marriage and Divorce, which I personally believe only should be between a man and a woman, and is also extremely important in that families are really what tends to hold Society together.** Here again, some of these questions might be pertinent to your life, others maybe not. Only consider those questions that are meaningful to you, which might take only one sitting, or more. But it might be helpful if these questions were reviewed by the participants a week before they're discussed to see what is of interest to them. **I Cor. 11:3-16, I Tim 2:8-15, Gal 3:26-28, Etc..**

QUESTIONS

1. Should women be given equal opportunity along with men in employment in all cases? What about the military? What about sports? If not, explain.

2. Should women receive equal pay for equal work alongside men?

3. Do you feel one should lower the quality standards in a certain situation solely to prevent gender discrimination?

4. Who has the major responsibility for nurturing a child in a marriage; or financially supporting the home: The man or the woman? Why?

   A) What is the prime purpose of a marriage?
   B) What are the economic factors that could affect your conception of what a marriage arrangement should be, and what could be done to change this situation, if it needs changing?

C) What are the career interest factors that could affect your conception of what a marriage arrangement should be, and what could be done to change this situation, if it needs changing?

5. Are the woman's major responsibilities in life to have children and take care of the home?

6. What are the physical and emotional differences between men and women that might effect one's role in life?

7. What might be the role of a woman in Church? What about ordination to any of the following offices: Deacon, Elder, Pastor, Priest or Bishop?

8. If man were to rule over woman at the beginning of time because woman came from man according to Genesis 2:21-23, why did God say that man should rule over woman after the Fall (Gen 3:16)?

    A) Could you say that man and woman became equal or helpmates once again after the death and resurrection of Jesus Christ (Gal 3:28)?

9. Could one of the reasons why Jesus only chose men as Apostles be that even though the Gospels are in the New Testament, they are really part of the Old Testament whereby women were still thought to be submissive to men as a result of the Fall?

10. Doesn't being the head and being submissive in and of itself create an inequality?

11. In reading Paul's letters, should you consider that everything that Paul wrote as being a universal truth, or should you distinguish within his writings what's universal and what's locally situational?

12. If women are treated more as unique individuals, instead of as sex objects, would this lessen the need for pornographic scenarios some men have. or more importantly, sexual crimes some men commit, such as rape or sexual slavery?

13. Do you feel that polygamy is really unfair to women?

14. Do you believe that as more and more churches use ordained women clergy, women clergy would be more acceptable within Christian religious circles?

15. As more and more churches tend to accept women clergy, do you feel Christianity offers women more equality than any other major world religion?

16. Do you feel a woman pastor could more effectively counsel a women counselee than a male pastor could? Why, or why not?

17. Do you feel that if more and more Christians experience the pastoral leadership qualities that some women seem to possess, that women clergy ordination would become less and less of a divisive issue within the Christian Church?

18. Do you feel one should never be judged solely by gender as to what one can or can not do in life? I do, but what do you think?

19. Why are there so many divorces taking place in today's society? And what can or should we do about this? Should one concentrate more on preparing oneself for the Wedding or the Marriage?

20. Should Priests be allowed to marry? Why or Why not?

21 Should marriage only be between a man and a women? Why or Why not?

22. What should one do to prepare oneself for marriage? And what are some of the questions that a mate should consider asking in choosing another mate on A) Personality, B) Religion, C) Health, D) Companionship (most important), E) Attitudes about Sex, F) Family, G) Humour, H) Ambition, I) Money, J) Empathy, K) Marriage, and L) Children? In doing this, should one have extensive counselling sessions before marriage in dealing with these issues? One should also realize that one's attitude toward money is the # 1 issue that tends to break up couples. See Supplement #1 for more details.

23. Could you define what love really is?

Supplement # 1A

RELATIONSHIP BUILDING WHICH SHOULD BE DONE WITH A COLD AND ANALYTICAL APPROACH. ONE HAS TO DISTINGUISH BETWEEN INFATUATION, OR ROMANTIC LOVE, WHICH IS THE MERGING OF TWO INDIVIDUALS INTO ONE, AND TRUE LOVE, WHICH IS DISCOVERING OURSELVES AS TWO SEPARATE INDIVIDUALS SEEKING A COMMITTED RELATIONSHIP.

QUESTIONS TO ASK YOURSELF ABOUT YOUR PARTNER THAT COULD HELP BUILD A STRONG RELATIONSHIP, IF YOU CAN LIVE WITH THE ANSWERS

A) Personality Traits
1) has good taste in choice of clothes. 2) has no unattractive nervous habits. 3) makes too much of neatness and cleanliness. 4) pays attention to personal appearance. 5) strives to keep promises. 6) tries to be on time to keep engagements. 7) has sleep and work habits I like. 8) has food and drink habits like mine. 9) is a calm person. 10) is an efficient person. 11) has

standards I honestly admire. 12) is an interesting and stimulating companion. 13) is at ease in social conversation. 14) has good manners. 15) considers the feelings of others.

B) Religion
16) believes too strongly that the church knows best in all things. 17) feels that his or her religion is superior or inferior to mine. 18) lives according to his or her religious beliefs. 19) wants our social life to center around the church. 20) is against the church. 21) believes and feels as I do about religion. 22) is a religious person. 23) accepts all religious views as good. 24) wants to argue about religion. 25) is set in religious ways and will not change. 26) thinks we will be unhappy unless we agree on religion

C) Health
27) worries about his or her health. 28) is in good physical health. 29) is in good emotional health. 30) needs medical care to maintain good health. 31) has close relatives who are mentally ill. 32) has close relatives who are deformed or retarded.

D) Companionship
33) enjoys being with me. 34) is interested and likes most of the things I like. 35) enjoys and is at ease with the people I like. 36) likes and gets along with children. 37) feels we must have the same interests and always be together. 38) has a hobby or sport I do not like. 39) has interests and activities I can't share. 40) prefers many people to small groups. 41) would rather travel than stay at home. 42) prefers a quiet evening with me to parties.

E) Sex
43) sees sex as more than physical love. 44) knows that both men and women have need for sexual self expression. 45) thinks of sex as a wholesome part of life. 46) wants to have sex relations before we marry. 47) gives and returns physical expressions of affection. 48) feels that the opposite sex is inferior or superior. 49) will be happy to limit his or her sex activities to one partner. 50) will need sexual relations more than I. 51) has a different understanding in what sexual relations mean in life. 52) attitudes toward masturbation,. 53) attitudes toward nudity.

F) Personality Traits II
54) faces our life together with confidence. 55) wants to be the important person in every activity. 56) must excel in an activity to enjoy it. 57) is dignified and formal. 58) is casual and informal. 59) maintains balance and emotional control in emergencies. 60) easily loses his or her temper—is impatient. 61) is a moody or depressive person. 62) is an anxious person. 63) accepts disappointments and adjusts to change. 64) is at ease in many different social situations. 65) likes and is at ease with many different types of people. 66) looks forward to new experiences with pleasure.

G) Family
67) has a family that is more or less cultured and/or educated than mine. 68) has a family with more or less money than mine. 69) has more or less education than I. 70) has a family of higher or lower social standing than mine. 71) is liked and accepted by my father. 72) is liked and accepted by my mother. 73) is liked and accepted by my brothers and sisters. 74)

his or her father likes and accepts me. 75) his or her mother likes and accepts me. 76) his or her brothers and sisters likes and accepts me. 77) I do not like some members of his or her family. 78) he or she does not like some members of my family. 79) is of my race. 80) is a native of my country. 81) grew up in my neighborhood or in one like mine.

H) Humor
82) enjoys and sees humor in situations and jokes that are funny to me. 83) considers the feelings of others in telling jokes and stories. 84) can take and enjoy a joke at his or her own expense. 85) has a "life of the party" personality. 86) enjoys crude and offensive jokes and stories. 87) joins in the fun and humor at parties.

I) Ambition
88) is willing to work hard for success. 89) lives from day to day without plans for the future. 90) believes that "connections" are most important for success. 91) is sacrificing too much for the future. 92) is unable to work for distant goals. 93) has reasonable and possible life goals. 94) would like to succeed without having to work. 95) feels that money and what it buys are the important proofs of success. 96) has ability and training to achieve the success he or she wants. 97) lives mainly for professional success. 98) lives mainly for social success.

J) Money
99) worries about spending money for pleasure.. 100) spends money with no thought about the future. 101) is or would be unhappy without money for luxuries and costly pleasures. 102) spends his or her money for selfish reasons. 103) makes good use of his or her money. 104) is realistic in saving and planning for the future. 105) has money but will not spend it. 106) is happy with what he or she can afford to buy. 107) enjoys spending money to help others. 108) tries to buy love or friendship. 109) may find it difficult to live within our income.

K) Empathy
110) believes in me and in my love. 111) shares and discusses his or her problems with me. 112) understands me and sympathizes with my feelings. 113) listens to and helps me solve my problems. 114) tries to change habits and behavior I do not like. 115) is a dependent person. 116) has more or less energy and enthusiasm than I. 117) is more or less optimistic than I. 118) takes advantage of me and uses me. 119) is considerably older or younger than I. 120) tries to dominate me and control me. 121) is possessive or a jealous person. 122) expects me to play a dependent role. 123) accepts me as I am. 124) is considerably taller or shorter than I.

L) Marriage
125) will treat me as his or her equal in marriage. 126) thinks of marriage as a sacrifice of freedom. 127) will enjoy an independent life in his or her own home. 128) avoids making definite plans for marriage. 129) wants me to replace his or her mother or father. 130) has a mother or father who wants to make all our important decision. 131) believes marriage will solve our problems. 132) is ready for the responsibilities of marriage including children. 133) may want to escape from an unpleasant home or other problems by marriage. 134) wants to live with or near his or her family. 135) thinks of marriage as an opportunity for mutual growth. 136) believes we cannot be happy unless there is as much romance in our marriage

as in our courtship. 137) feels the man has to be in control in a marriage. 138) Is in general agreement on how many children we should have and how to raise them.

And finally in a relationship between a man and woman, one should realize that, in general, initially the man's primary focus is on a physical sexual relationship (not thinking of having children), whereas a woman's primary focus is on an emotional sexual relationship with the possibility of having children at some point, and both parties have to accept these differences if this relationship is to grow. After all, children will be the future here on earth.

And just to reiterate, the most confrontational issue that seems to divide couples is their attitudes toward money-

Supplement # 1B

WHY DO SO MANY TRADITIONAL MARRIAGES FAIL?
By
Corbin M. Wright

In the olden days we seemed to have much more stability in our traditional marriages because the roles of the husband and wife were specifically understood. The husband was to earn the money to support the family materially, while the wife was to take care of the home and children as they come along. Today with the emancipation of women to pursue other careers of their choice, besides that of homemaker, traditional marriages have suffered. That is because the roles of husband and wife have now overlapped and became intermingled with each other, so that traditional marriages have become much more complex, and because of the reluctance of many men to accept their new roles in marriages.. Now I'm all for this emancipation of women, because women too are educated, other than in being a housewife or mother, and they too should be able to pursue the dream of their career choice as well, if it's not that of a homemaker, so I feel the dynamics and understanding of traditional marriages have to change. And this I feel is what we're struggling with today, but I also feel that in the future, if we haven't already done so, we will be able to fine ways to share our responsibilities in a fairer and a much more equitable way so that we will continue to have successful, although more complex, traditional marriages.

Of course, making divorce easier and easier today doesn't help either. In fact, today divorce has become much easier to attain because women now have become much more financially independent, so that they can live independently from a husband. We also want to give couples a fair option to get out of a marriage if they feel they really shouldn't be married. The problem here is that in many cases we don't give the couple enough time to see if the marriage could really work out or not, especially if children are involved.

Of course before traditional marriages do take place, the bride and groom have to understand the differences between infatuation and true love. Of course to begin a relationship between a man and a woman you need infatuation, whereby both parties are attracted to each other in some way, but eventually you will find that this infatuation will tend to fade away if you just depend upon that. So before matrimony really takes place, true love between the two parties has to start to develop whereby both parties can start to accept what imperfections they might encounter in their mate. And this sometimes can be very difficult to do. (See previous Document on Relationships – Supplement 1A)

But then you'll start to get to know each other as a true Spiritual human being with all the imperfections and perfections being exposed, and you as a couple will start to become much more compatible with each other. And as a result your children will greatly benefit from all of this because they will then see a stability in their own lives, that you find lacking in so many of the other families in the world today, and then these children can focus more fervently on the true purpose, as they or God sees it, in their own lives.

"WOMEN" AND "MARRIAGE"

THIS PAGE SHOULD BE USED TO WRITE ANSWERS TO THOSE QUESTIONS IN THIS CHAPTER IN WHICH YOU'RE INTERESTED. IF NECESSARY, USE ADDITIONAL PAPER.

Chapter 7

HOW TO DEAL WITH HOMOSEXUALS

It was reported that Abraham Lincoln once said that "I don't like that person very much, so I must get to know him better". This must be the attitude of Christians concerning those people that are disliked by any Christian, and most Christians have a strong dislike for Homosexuals. In fact, Homosexuality is one of the biggest and most explosive issues facing the Church today. So even though most of us as Christians feel that Homosexuality is a sin because of all the negativity of Homosexuality found in the Bible, we have to talk with them in a calm and empathetic way to find out where they came from, and how they discovered they were gay because eventually you might find Homosexuals and Homosexual couples coming to our churches and looking for acceptance. That's why engaging in this discussion questionnaire is so important for Christians. This would hopefully help Christian understand where Homosexuals might be coming from. After all, we're all children of God . Now again some of these questions might be pertinent to your life, others maybe not. Only consider those questions that are meaningful to you, which might take only one sitting, or more. But it might be helpful if these questions were reviewed by the participants a week before they're discussed to see what is of interest to them. **Gen. 1 & 2, Lev. 18:22, 20:13, Rom. 1:26-27, Etc..**

Questions

A) How to Interact with Homosexuals

1. Most Christians believe that homosexuality is a sin, but believe that one should only condemn the sin and not the sinner. Unfortunately in condemning the sin, denigrating language that many Christians use in doing this, is perceived by many as condemning the sinner as well. This, I believe, sometimes lead extremists to do a great deal of violence against the gays, which is not right. Therefore I feel we Christians have to be very sensitive as to what language (other than calling it a sin) we use in describing this activity. What do you think? Besides we have to realize that most homosexuals that we come in contact with are usually not violent because, on a personal note, I just said "No thanks" on 3 different occasions in my lifetime when I was propositioned by 3 gays; and I had no problem.

2. If a homosexual, who was unrepentant as to his or her sexual orientation, came into your church, how would you relate to that person? Would your relationship be

different if you met that homosexual under different circumstances? Does God really hate gays?

3. Do you feel that the AIDS epidemic was caused by God as a result of His anger over all the homosexual activity that's taking place in the world today? Do you feel safe sex is the answer to this, if you can define what safe sex is? What about condoms? And what about Lesbians and AIDS?

4. Do you believe that we should defend the Civil Rights of homosexuals in all cases? E.G. As a teacher, in sports, in the military, or in the Church ministry? If not, explain..

5. If you don´t approve of a homosexual (practicing) being a member of the clergy, what do you think should be done to a person who has demonstrated his or her faithful service in a superb manner to the ministry over a long period of time, but has just recently been discovered to be a practicing homosexual over that same tenure?.

6. Should homosexuals have the right to marry? If not, because marriage should only be between a man and a woman, but could a homosexual marriage fall under the remaining definition of a marriage, and perhaps be called something else? What should parents do when they have to choose between Christ or their children, if the children are involved in a homosexual marriage? See Supp # 1

7. Should homosexuals be allowed to adopt children? If not, because children should have gender role models to follow, but wouldn´t it be more important to have human role models to emulate? And what about single people adopting? One might than say that the children might eventually emulate their parent's sexual behaviour if adopted, but this depends on what actually causes homosexuality. What do you think?

8. Someone once said that we all have some homosexual tendencies within us but in most of us they're not dominant. Do you agree?

9. If one wants to get rid of a dominant homosexual trait or sin, what can one do?

B) How to deal with Homosexuality

10. In the Old Testament God states that homosexuality is a sin, but He never gives a reason for this dictum. Why do you think He gave us this commandment? Do you possibly believe that this activity is designated as a sin here only because it breaks the first commandment God ever gave us, which is "to go and multiply" (Gen 1:28)? (This still seems to be the Roman Catholic position). Of course today with overpopulation and poverty in many different places, conditions have changed; and with birth control being more acceptable, this commandment seems not to be so absolute anymore. What do you think?

11. In the Bible, does the Sodom and Gomorrah story condemn homosexuality, or only homosexual gang rape?

12. In the Gospels Jesus never mentions a concern about homosexuality being a sin, but He does mention that He doesn't intend to change any part of the law one iota, but only to fulfill it. What does Jesus mean by this? Is He just referring to the ten commandments, the Spirit of the Law, or to more than that since we feel much of the Law that one finds throughout the Old Testament, such as certain dietary laws, don't apply to us anymore?

13. In Paul's letters, homosexuality is condemned in several places, but especially in Romans 1:26-27 where this activity is actually defined. Is this definition all-inclusive in that it covers all homosexual activity? Paul's homosexual definition: Lustful and Unnatural

    A) Can any homosexual activity ever be loving?

    B) Can any homosexual activity ever be natural in the sense that you're born with it? If you can answer "Yes" to either of the above questions, it means that Paul's definition is definitely not all-inclusive. What do you think?

14. What do you think causes most homosexuality: birth, early upbringing, easier to relate to same gender, or conscious choice?

15. Would God create someone with a dominant homosexual trait, and then turn around and condemn that trait He made as being sinful?

16. If a person were having trouble with his or her homosexuality, what would you suggest to that person?

17. If a homosexual were having some other type of problem and came to you for help, how would you deal with his or her homosexuality? Or would you have to?

18. Does a homosexual need to change his or her sexual activity orientation to be saved?

19. To help pinpoint the cause of homosexuality, however, I feel that there should be much more dialogue with homosexuals to determine how they seemed to discover their own sexual orientation. What do you think? And what about Bisexuality and Transvestites?

20. Someone once said that a heterosexual couple is a more complete couple in the sense that this is the only type of couple that can reproduce offspring, and that can think more comprehensively in that men and women actually think differently. How do you feel about this? And is this the reason that one might call homosexuality a sin, because if Homosexuality tends to become permanent, it doesn't create the perfect

relationship between man and woman that God intended for us all to have, to fully enjoy His creation (Gen 2)? See Supp. # 2.

A pastor who is a strong Gay Rights Advocate feels that Homosexuality is just another Human trait, such as being Left-handed or Right-handed, and if this conflicts with the Bible, than Science should rule.

Supplement 1

GAY MARRIAGE
by

Corbin M. Wright

I have a friend who is a Gay Pastor who strongly believes in Gay Marriage and believes that Gays are developed genetically. He further states that Scientists have proven this, even though they haven't found any Homosexual Genes as of yet. He says this is because it's the same reasoning that can be applied as to why some people are right-handed, while others are left-handed. Scientists believe this is genetically caused as well according to my friend. And legalizing Gay Marriage seems like the culmination in my friend's efforts to equalize Gay Rights with the Rights of any other individual.

I personally don't believe that Scientists have proved that Gays are Genetically determined. I believe that Scientists have assumed Gays are Genetically determined which means that they probably are, even though they haven't found any Homosexual Genes in them as proof of this. They believe this because they can't seem to determine any other reason why a person is Gay. This also holds true as to why a person is right-handed or left-handed. In other words, this is all assumed, but not really proven.

Now Gays are probably Genetically determined originally, but I'm afraid that as Homosexuality becomes more and more accepted as being normal in some people, some Heterosexuals will tend to be attracted to Homosexuality because for some Heterosexuals, attraction to someone of the same gender is easier to deal with than someone from a different gender. And this tendency could increase as Homosexuality tends to be understood as being completely normal. Therefore in the future I believe you can find that Homosexuality can be caused genetically, and environmentally as well.

Now I'm all for Gay Rights as far as Individuals are concerned, but I would not include Marriage between two Gays as being one of them. You could call it something else if you want, but Marriage, I believe, should only be between a man and a woman (Gen 2). After all, according to Gen 2, God's intention seems to be that the only couples God was interested in creating were those between a man and a woman. So in a sense, Gay Marriage sounds Anti-Biblical. I say this also because a Gay couple is really not equal to a Heterosexual couple. For example, a Gay couple can not produce children, and a

Gay couple can not think as comprehensively as a Heterosexual couple can because men and women think differently, and a Heterosexual couple do make for a more complete thinking unit.

I would appreciate very much any comment you would care to make on this article. Thank you very much.

Various Comments on the above Article by a number of Pastors.

1) I agree .with the Article

2) When it comes to the issue of human sexuality, I admit ignorance: I do not understand enough about same-sex relationships to form an opinion on their morality and ethical good. Is it nature or nurture? Is it genetic or learned/conditioned? I don't know. Nor do I think I am alone in my ignorance.

I am now and have always been oriented and attracted to the opposite sex. I am a devout heterosexual. Therefore, it's difficult for me to get my head wrapped around the idea of same-sex relations, much less empathize with those who do. Frankly, I would rather not know what goes on between the sheets of two consenting adults. As a minister, I am more concerned about the quality of the relationship between two people rather than 'who's-sticking-what-where'.

To complicate matters, I don't think that human sexuality can be divided neatly and cleanly between as an 'either-or' proposition, specifically, either heterosexual or homosexual. Maybe the title of the book *Fifty Shades of Grey* serves as a useful metaphor to describe a sliding scale of human sexuality. I am probably at one extreme end of the spectrum. But I can imagine that sliding along the scale, one finds practicing heterosexuals who may fantasize about same-sex relations. Then there are bisexuals in the middle of the spectrum, with devout homosexuals occupying the other end of the range. Then there is the question of celibates—are they on the scale or not? This then begs the question of whether sexuality is an action or an ideation (orientation). For example, if one is celibate, but fantasizes about same-sex relations, then is the person a homosexual or not? Who gets to decide that question—the celibate or society?

I have less difficulty with the Christian understanding of marriage. Jesus seems to define marriage as between a man and a woman (Mark 10:6-9; Matthew 19:4-12). So, from the church's standpoint, we 'marry' men to woman, and women to men.

How the State defines marriage is a matter of passing interest to the Church, but not dispositive. The State's business is the State's business, and the Church's business is the Church's business. The Church is not bound to acknowledge, much less honor, any decision of the State to license same-sex marriages. This is because Church's do not license, but rather solemize and sanction the joining together of a man and a woman.

But I ask: Are there other ways to celebrate and acknowledge formally, as the Church, the commitment of a man to a man, or a woman to a woman? I watched a television program the other evening entitled *Vikings* wherein a man swore fealty to the chieftain (the earl). It was a public profession of loyalty and devotion from one man to another, even unto death. And the public received and acknowledged that commitment as good for the community. Granted, a man swearing to a king has vertical power built into the relationship, which is unlike the mutual and horizontal relationship of a marriage. But the public display of loyalty and devotion is what struck me as 'a good thing'. It bonded and forged a new relationship of trust and commitment.

Can and should the Church do the same with two men, or two women, who wish to make a similar pledge before God and the community? Not marriage, but something else. If God is a relationship within the Trinity, should we not also sanction and sanctify relationships between two people who want to make a public profession of their devotion to each other? It seems to me that such a pledge may be able to change the conversation somewhat. Instead of all this prurient talk about sex (about 'who's-sticking-what-where'), maybe we can focus on the meaning of relationships and its importance in our life of faith.

I probably provided more smoke than light with my musings above. Again, thank you for engaging me on this topic and for keeping me connected to the good folks down South.

3) : There is much in your statement of which I agree. Undeniably it is that the gay life style, encouraged by gay marriage, will give more environmental influence to romantic and sexual relations. But that trend goes with all the other dynamics that place ultimate value on the individual choice, preference, pleasure, etc. I preferred that marriage be retained for hetero couples and always thought that a new bonding relationship could celebrate gay life and connectedness, but we lost that battle so i now accept marriage for gays as a defacto reality. You point out that gay relationships may prove more attractive than straight because same gender relations are easier to handle is provocative, but probably open to much debate. Here at our church we have had lesbian couples, some legally married, for about a dozen years but are just about to welcome our first gay couple. We had them over yesterday for a welcome; wonderful couple with the older partner having been married, widowed and now legally married to his younger partner. One interesting phenomenon I observed is the number of previously men in straight marriages who when entering widower status convert or change or go with a same sex partner. That may validate your point. All very interesting and you certainly will get a lot of comment. Of course, the Argentine Govt is well advanced in fully accepting the gay reality, isn't it. I believe that this was one of several issues dividing the govt from the new Pope Francis.

4) I prefer to talk face to face about sensitive issues. I find myself in agreement with a great deal of what your pastor friend number 2 says. I don't think the old answers stand up so well anymore. I am very aware of what the Bible says, although as ever I would argue that it still needs to be viewed in its cultural context—there are after all a great many Biblical instructions that we do not directly follow, as we understand them in a different light now (in the OT dietary laws plus slavery guidance etc and in the NT things such as women should cover their heads and not speak in church etc. I am sure you are very familiar with all of this). Modern research does seem to indicate that our sexuality is a very complicated issue (as your friend correctly points out). From a pastoral context I can say that I have always had people

in my congregations that I have known are homosexual (both male and female) and that they have been some of the most committed and hard working Christians in those congregations. I find it hard to condemn them solely on the grounds that I do not share their sexual preference. I also find it hard to condemn loving and committed relationships. I do agree with your friend that the obsession with the sexual side is unhealthy and really no one else's business. I would also agree that maybe "marriage" is not an appropriate term to use—in England we use the term civil partnership, which has now become an accepted concept.

All in all, I think this is a very complicated issue. I am also not at all sure it is so important that the church should spend a great deal of time debating it rather than getting on with far clearer teachings, such as caring for the poor and needy and sharing God's love with those who need it.

5) The Catholic Church doesn't teach that homosexual *orientation* is a sin, but it does say that the orientation is disordered. So, the struggle is to try to articulate a position which simultaneously affirms the centrality of the traditional family while creating pastoral room for gay and lesbian Catholics.

6) Your article is very clear and concise. You've covered every key issue related to homosexualityin a respectful and wise way. I agree 100% with your thoughts. Thank very much for sharing.

7) I read your article with interest. I had never heard the excuse that homosexuality was a genetic presupposition. That is most interesting but a total deception.

God created us with a gender and a sexual orientation to match that gender. God is not confused nor is He conflicted about sexuality. He created us for pro creation not sexual deviance. In many ways this is not just an attack against morals and human sexuality, it is an attack against God Himself and His created order.

"God created man in His own image; in the image of God He created him; **male and female** *He created them. Then God blessed them, and God said to them, 'be fruitful and multiply; fill the earth and subdue it; have dominion over the fish of the sea, over the birds of the air, and over every living thing that moves on the earth." Genesis 1:27, 28*

God created Adam and Eve, not *"Adam and Steve"*. God created them as an opposite pair to have a loving sexual union for pro creation. To continue the work of God's creation upon the earth. Never in God's creation were sexual deviance and rebellion against God's order accepted. As far back as the flood and then Sodom and Gomorrah, God clearly showed his displeasure and righteous judgement against such behavior.

Jude 1:7 could not be more clear:

". . . Sodom and Gomorrah, and the cities around them in a similar manner to these, having given themselves over to sexual immorality and gone after strange flesh, are set forth as an example, suffering the vengeance of eternal fire."

God clearly records these events in scripture as a warning to those who are to come to not repeat the same sins and abominations.

*"Professing to be wise, they became fools . . . . therefore God also gave them up to uncleanness, in the lusts of their hearts, to dishonour their bodies among themselves, who exchanged the truth of God for the lie, and worshiped and served the creature rather than the Creator, who is blessed forever. Amen. For this reason God gave them up to vile passions. For even their **women exchanged the natural use for what is against nature.** Likewise also the **men, leaving the natural use of the woman, burned in their lust for one another, men with men committing what is shameful,** and receiving in themselves the penalty of their error which was due. And even as they did not like to retain God in their knowledge, **God gave them over to a debased mind, to do those things which are not fitting.**" Romans 1:22-28*

This is the New Testament and cannot be easily discounted or done away with unless you want to discount the whole canon of scripture which would indeed be dangerous. We cannot just pick and choose the scriptures that we like and discard the rest at our pleasure or discretion.

If you don't adhere to Scripture (or(my interpretation of Scripture, author's note), it could affect your Eternal Salvation.

8) I will not pretend to offer an impartial opinion, since according to my theology/philosophy only an infinite God knows all and can be impartial—the rest of us "know in part" and hence are partial from the perspective of our limited knowledge. We can, however, seek to be well-informed, listening to all sides and be fair, not ruling out valid evidence/arguments from anyone just because we disagree with their conclusions. So in evaluating opinions it is important to weigh them, not just count them. The opinion of 100 people who simply reflect the ignorance and prejudices of their culture only counts in democratic elections, not in the pursuit of truth. Since heterosexist and homophobic church members usually know nothing about church history in this area, they will not be aware of the significance of the fact that the Sodom story was the main basis for condemning "sodomites" to death for more than 1000 years, and that the citations of 1 Cor 6 and 1 Tim 1 condemning "homosexuals" has been developed only in recent decades, based on a new false translation, with the collapse of the argument based on Biblical references to Sodom.

Many people, like you, for family reasons, etc. seek to maintain relationship with homophobic churches. Although it is a bit like consuming regular meals with "poison in the pot," if you can handle it, there are advantages and the possibility of being an agent of education and change in the world-wide denominational "trench warfare," which gradually we Gays are winning. However, for your spiritual welfare, if it is possible at the same time to seek out alternative spiritual input, from a Metropolitan Community Church or similar gay-positive Christian ministries, the extra vitamins encourage healthy survival in a hostile environment. If you succeed in developing a good same-sex relationship and enjoy spiritual fellowship in an encouraging context, probably your fear that homosexuality is a sin will evaporate. Knowing that "God is love" and experiencing authentic human love are fundamental, and the only canonical book dedicated to human sexuality, Song of Songs, refers continually to sexual relations outside any framework of marriage and with no concern for procreation.

Regarding gay marriage, the Hebrew Bible heroes were mainly polygamous, wise Solomon even with 700 wives and 300 concubines, while the New Testament (Jesus and Paul) recommended avoiding heterosexual marriage (which implied children), being "eunuchs for the sake of the Kingdom" to leave maximum freedom for Kingdom proclamation in itinerant ministries, so neither Testament really supports the modern emphasis on the heterosexual nuclear family. Neither Testament ever refers to "families" (despite sloppy modern translations) but to patriarchal "houses/households" commonly with 50-100 persons and many slaves. 1 Timothy probably comes from a disciple of Paul communicating something of his teaching to a later generation and different context; hence it contradicts what Paul himself counseled about widows not remarrying (1 Cor 7).

Various comments on the above Article by a number of Lay Persons

1) This is a very good article, but personally to me it is a subject that hurts.

I understand that in freedom anyone can live with anyone they please, abiding by the laws, but I too believe that Marriage is between a man and a woman.

I believe we of the older generation feel that things are changing maybe much faster than we really like.

2) I am completely in favour of gay "civil union", as it is called in Argentina.

I will tell you why.

Homosexuals have always been discriminated against in society but, ironically, in many cases they are more open and honest than many others who appear to be "normal". I think that God expects us to be honest and not to pretend to do something just because that way society will accept us.

It is absolutely necessary that this "civil union" is a legal right, in my opinion.

Discrimination for homosexuals usually start in their own family, being the father who usually hates the "weird son" or "weird daughter" because of what people (society) will think of this. Therefore, these sons and daughters are sadly rejected and in many, many cases, they are even turned out of their home.

After this, the homosexuals may meet someone who really loves them, who really cares about them, no matter what their sexuality, and that person remains by their side for the rest of their lives.

Now, if the "civil union" does not exist, when this homosexual passes away, his or her money goes directly to his or her parents, yes, the ones that rejected him or her in the first place, probably calling his or her homosexuality a "disgrace" for the family. Now, if the "civil union" exists, then the money goes to the partner, yes, that other homosexual who really loved him or her and was there for him or her for years.

I only find that this last situation is fair and that God would approve of this.

Also most of us are heterosexuals and will remain so, no matter how open people will be about homosexuality.

3) I believe that Homosexuality is a social disease, such as in Alcoholism. I'm disgusted with it.

4) I believe in Gay Marriage, because without Gay Marriage, Gays would never have the same rights that other married individuals would have. Also I believe the message of Jesus will trump Leviticus or any other Book of the Bible.

CONCLUSTION: It's true, as one pastor said, that caring for the concerns of the poor and needy and sharing the love of God with those who need it, is much more important, but at the same time we shouldn't just shove this issue under the rug as so many churches seem to be doing, because eventually most churches would experience Gay couples visiting them and looking for acceptance, so we have to start understanding them. And we do need to discuss this issue more fully to understand what Christianity is all about.

Supplement # 2

IS HOMOSEXUALITY REALLY A SIN? by
Corbin M. Wright
Graduate from New York Theological Seminary
corbinw@hotmail.com

Most Christians believe that it is, and most Christians point to Romans 1 in Scripture to indicate that it is. In Romans 1 it does say that Homosexuality is a sin because it is lustful and unnatural. But then you have to ask yourself this question: Can two homosexuals ever be in a sexual loving relationship? In my imagination, I believe that they can be, although I don't understand it. So I believe that you also have to ask yourself this question?

I don't know what really causes Homosexuality within a person, but Scripturally speaking, I believe that the most significant Biblical verse to determine whether Homosexuality in a sin or not, is not Romans 1, but Genesis 2. In Genesis it states that man and woman should hang on to one another and become one. God never said that man should hang on to man, or that woman should hang on to woman, but that man should hang on to woman. Therefore, it seems that couples, if they are going to commit themselves completely to each other and forever here on earth, should follow God's intention. And it seems clear here that God's only intention was to create couples that were made up of a man and a woman. Anything else would be a sin because it would be against God's intention..

Now why would this be true? What are the advantages of couples made up of a man and woman over those just made up of men or women. 1) Those couples made up of a man and a woman are the only ones that can create another Human Being, and 2) men and women think differently, and those couples made up of one man and one women would create a more comprehensive thinking unit. And this is the type of Perfection that God wants us to reach. Anything other than Perfection in this regard is Sin, and any approach in life that leads us away from attaining this Perfection is Sin, unless there is a genetic deficiency involved.

Now in a way I can understand why one might chose Homosexuality over Heterosexuality when one sees how many marriages break up throughout society. Why get involved in that type of merry-go-round, especially when children are involved. Also it is much easier to relate to someone of one's own gender because you tend to think alike and this makes it much easier to form a loving relationship, plus you normally don't have to think about children unless you want to adopt some. It's much easier this way. So we have to be somewhat empathetic with Homosexuals and try to understand where they're coming from. After all, they're Children of God also. This is my opinion. What do you think?

HOMOSEXUALITY

**THIS PAGE SHOULD BE USED TO WRITE ANSWERS TO THOSE
QUESTIONS IN THIS CHAPTER IN WHICH YOU'RE INTERESTED.
IF NECESSARY, USE ADDITIONAL PAPER.**

Chapter 8

HOW TO POSSIBLY RESOLVE THE ABORTION ISSUE

Is the fetus a human being or a potential human being? This is the central question in regard to allowing abortions to take place. What does the Bible say about this? Does the Bible really answer this question, or not? Hopefully these questions below might help in answering this concern. For example, if you would consider the fetus as being a human being, you probably would find no circumstances in which you would allow an abortion to take place, except perhaps to save the life of the mother.. If, however you find the fetus to be a potential human being your options would be much more open. The problem here is that if you allow no abortions, you most likely would find many more unwanted babies being born however much you dislike this consequence, creating much more of an anti-social behaviour coming from these unwanted off-spring as they mature into adulthood. The answer has to be by finding some way to make these unwanted babies wanted, or by finding ways in which to prevent unwanted pregnancies from happening in the first place. These questions hopefully will also help resolve some of these concerns. Here again, some of these questions might be pertinent to your life, others maybe not. Only consider those questions that are meaningful to you, which might take only one sitting, or more. But it might be helpful if these questions were reviewed by the participants a week before they're discussed to see what is of interest to them. **Gen 1:27, Ex. 20:13, Jer. 1:5, Ecl 4:1-3, Nu.3:15, Etc.**

Questions

1. When do you believe that human life really begins?

2. Does the Bible suggest when life actually begins? Where? Especially if

   A) In Psalm 139.13-16 it indicates that God is very much involved in our creation, but not that the fetus is actually a human being.

   B) In Jeremiah 1:4-5 it indicates that God knew Jeremiah before he was conceived suggesting that if you consider the fetus as being a human being, it must have been a human being before conception.

   C) In Ecclesiastes 4:1-3 it suggests it might be better to abort fetuses than to cause one to live a miserable life.

D) In Numbers 3:15.a census was taken of those who were only over 1 month old indicating that fetuses were perhaps not considered human beings in Biblical times.

3. So considering these above Biblical verses, when do you think that the soul actually connects with the body, or can you actually separate the body and soul? If you can't separate the body from the soul, wouldn't the soul also die when the body dies? And then where does eternal life fit in? What does the Bible actually say? Do you think that your personality might be your soul?

4. Is a fetus a human being with all the moral attributes or a potential human being where you are not even conscious of all your moral attributes? Can Science prove when Human Life really begins? What does Scripture say about this? If a fetus has all of its moral attributes at conception, does it have to be conscious of it to be considered a human being?

5. Do you believe in absolutely no abortions for anyone regardless of the circumstances?

6. If your answer is "No" to question number 4, what might be some of the exceptions as suggested below?

   A) Save the Life of the Mother
   B) Rape
   C) Incest
   D) Deformity of Fetus
   E) Economic Reasons
   F) Mental Instability
   G) Having In-depth counselling
   H) Other
   I) Abortion on Demand

7. If a woman's choice on abortion were severely limited, wouldn't there be a danger of having many more unhealthy illegal abortions, especially among the poor? And wouldn't there be more unwanted children being born, causing much more potential future social unrest? What do you think?

8. To avoid this sometimes violent confrontational approach of abortion or no-abortion, wouldn't it be better to develop a dialogical approach whereby both sides could try and discover ways to altar conditions in society so unwanted pregnancies would no longer be a problem, thereby eliminating the desire for abortions? How would you do this? Or would it be better to bomb abortion clinics and/or kill abortion activists as an answer?

9. Would emphasizing abstinence (perfect safe sex) be a satisfactory solution for all to avoid abortions until one is married or ready to have children? If not, and one has a

strong sexual drive, would sublimation (substituting a nonsexual activity for a sexual one) be a satisfactory solution for all?

10. Would one way to altar conditions in society, so unwanted children would no longer be a problem, be to improve the economic situations of families, or to help them find a more meaningful purpose in life? How would you do this?

11. Would you support disseminating all birth control information available and means with instruction on use, that are medically safe, and the availability on sterilization in certain cases, to anyone, as an answer in preventing most unwanted pregnancies so that the issue of abortion would never even have to be considered?

12. Would better and more streamlined adoption procedures facilitate solutions as to what to do with unwanted children, such as lessening financial requirements, eliminating unnecessary red tape, and being less concerned with the single, gay, cultural, ethnical, or racial match-ups, as long as you find that the child will receive the love and essential protection in a family-setting he or she needs?

13. If marriage is the ideal situation to raise wanted children, should divorce be prohibited? Under what conditions, if any, should divorce and remarriage be granted where it affects children? Would trial marriages or unofficial cohabitation, which more and more people are using today, be the answer to so many divorces and in helping raise children? Or would pre-marital in-depth psychological counselling be more of an answer?

14. Do you feel intimate communal living arrangements would be more helpful in raising wanted children?

15. Would you support a community sexual education program set up for all ages to cover all aspects of sexual behaviour, so people can have a greater understanding in the role sexuality should play in one's life, as a means for lessening the desire of abortion?

16. If sublimation, or even Biblical directives toward abstinence don´t work, and you sense that there is a strong risk of one having sexual intercourse, which potentially could create more unwanted children for the abortion knife, would encouraging some sexual activity for both genders be helpful, such as in individualistic masturbation, or mutual masturbation (Females can do this also), where there's no danger of unwanted pregnancies or sexual diseases? And in the future, would you find that sexual virtual reality on the computer might be the answer? What do you think about all of this?

17. Do you feel that the more one finds equal opportunities for both men and women in society whereby women might not be treated as mere sex objects, the less one will find a need for abortions?

18. How can one improve communications between family loved ones, if one party finds herself in an unwanted pregnancy situation whereby abortion seems to be the only answer?

19. Would excessive sexual attractiveness of the opposite gender that could lead to unwanted pregnancies, be minimized, if we could get to the point in our life where we're not ashamed or embarrassed to appear nude in mixed company in any individual-chosen situation? The author experienced this positive phenomenon while actively participating in a nudist camp for 3 years many years ago, and also a movement in the US is now taking place in promoting social nudism among teenagers to eliminate the mystery of gender nakedness that drive many to premature sex. What do you think about all this?

20. What other ways might you suggest on preventing unwanted pregnancies and causing unwanted children to become wanted so abortion or no abortion wouldn't even be an issue anymore?

I feel that the best way to stop this confrontational approach to abortion or no abortion is to find ways to prevent unwanted pregnancies, and secondly, if this doesn't work, to find ways to make these unwanted pregnancies or children, wanted. What do you think? Otherwise you're going to have much more anti-social behaviour committed by these unwanted offspring in the future.

ABORTION

THIS PAGE SHOULD BE USED TO WRITE ANSWERS TO THOSE QUESTIONS IN THIS CHAPTER IN WHICH YOU'RE INTERESTED. IF NECESSARY, USE ADDITIONAL PAPER.

_____

_____

_____

_____

_____

_____

_____

_____

_____

_____

_____

_____

_____

_____

_____

_____

_____

_____

_____

_____

_____

_____

_____

_____

Chapter 9

CHRISTIANITY AND OTHER RELIGIONS

Why are you a Christian and what difference does it make if you decided to change to another religion or belief? This discussion would focus on the differences and similarities between Christianity and other World Religions, such as Judaism, Islamism, Buddhism, Hinduism, and some of the lesser known religions, **and how one as a Christian should deal with these other Beliefs. This discussion would also zero in on the possibility of developing a World Religion, or rejecting religion all together. And finally it reflects on what the interpretation of your faith might be if life were discovered on other planets.** Here again, some of these questions might be pertinent to your life, others maybe not. Only consider those questions that are meaningful to you, which might take only one sitting, or more. But it might be helpful if these questions were reviewed by the participants a week before they're discussed to see what is of interest to them. **John 8:31-47, Acts 4:8-12, Rom. 10:9-10, Etc.**

QUESTIONS

1. Define what you mean by Ecumenism, and do you believe in it? How would you relate to other religions?

2. What is a Christian? (See supplement-1 behind this questionnaire for a possible answer). Comment on the supplement and your opinion concerning the issue. Is there such a thing as an unconscious Christian?

3. Which do you believe is the prime purpose for the ten commandments: As a guide to show us how we should live, or as a tool to show us that in order for one to follow God's law one needs some outside help?

4. What is sin and how does Christianity deal with this phenomenon? And how does Christianity deal with Salvation?

5. Who is Jesus Christ, and how do we know that what we believe about Him is true or not? (See Supplement-2 and determine whether this reasoning is logical or not.).

6. How do you interpret the Bible, Literally or Contextually? And how do you know the Bible is true? (For a more complete analysis on the Bible see Supp. # 3)

7. Why don't the Jews accept Jesus Christ as the Messiah when he comes right out of their Old Testament prophecies? Did the Jews kill Jesus? What do the Jews do with sin? How do the Jews believe they are saved? How do you relate to the Jews? What can the Jews teach us?

8. How do you compare the Muslim's approach to God with the Christian's? What do the Muslims do with sin? How do the Muslims believe they are saved? How do you relate to the Muslims? What can the Muslims teach us?

9. How would you relate to the Muslim society? Do you feel God would ever instruct a believer to kill another because his or her belief is different? What do you believe is the purpose of the suicide bombers or honour killings? Do you believe God can accept this? And do you believe these suicide bombers really denigrate their religion to a Religion of Hate?

10. How do you feel about the way women are treated under the Muslim Belief?

11. How do you relate to the Black Muslims, and do they differ from the rest of the Muslims?

12. How do you compare the Hindu's approach to God with the Christian's? What do the Hindus do with sin? How do the Hindus believe they are saved? What can the Hindus teach us?

13. What do you think about reincarnation?

14. How do you compare the Buddhist's approach to God with the Christian's? What do the Buddhists do with sin? How do the Buddhists believe they are saved? What can the Buddhists teach us?

15. What do you think about Yoga or Transcendentalism?

16. How do you feel about Spiritualism? What do Spiritualists do with sin? And how do the Spiritualists feel we are saved? What can the Spiritualists teach us?

17. How do you feel about the worship of Satanism?

18. Why do you think there are a number of atheists and many agnostics in the world? How do you deal with human popularity in the world, if it conflicts with a God-given kindness?

19. Are these arguments as stated below a good reason to believe that a God does exist?

It's in the creation. It's illogical to assume that chance really created rationality, so since we were actually created with a desire for meaningfulness, which is a part of rationality and a creator is always greater than his creation, our creator must be greater

in personhood (a God) than we are. And our physical smallness compared to what's out there in the universe should be no criteria for our importance to God. After all, we do have rationality. Another argument for God's existence is that we being imperfect as we all know, but continually striving for perfection, must have developed this idea of perfection from someplace, and the most logical place that we developed this from seems to be from a higher power (a God, for instance). And finally, can you imagine a planet spinning around the universe in perfect unison allowing human life to evolve as it has for as long as it has without completely breaking up with all its earthquakes and volcanoes taking place without a God being in control.

20. Do you believe in astrology? What do you think this might teach us?

21. How do other religions not mentioned above, such as Taoism, Shintoism, Scientology, Universalism, or any ather religion you might think of, compare with Christianity? How do these religions handle sin? How do these religions handle Salvation? What can these religions teach us?

22. How do you feel about a World Religion whereby this World Religion just combines all the common doctrines that each of the separate religions possesses, and ignores the rest? What do you do with sin in this case? And how would a World Religion handle Salvation?

23. What do you do in regard to tolerance concerning other religions or other beliefs? How do you handle this? And how do you express your belief within the context of the other beliefs? Also which belief do you feel is most attractive and how do you feel you can convey this to others?

24. Would you be interested in working with an organization called "Good Samaritan Ministries"? This is a strong World-wide Evangelical Ecumenical Christian Organization that dedicates itself and counsels people, using relational techniques, who are suffering in some way, whether they are Christians, Jews, Muslims, Atheists, etc. This organization has been working very strongly in the Mideast, and is attempting to widen its scope where there are other conflicting issues arising among peoples. This organization tends to focus itself upon Human Rights, Much Prayer, and God's Will, with its ultimate goal being that they will hopefully find their answer in accepting Jesus Christ as their Lord & Savior. Contact goodsam@goodsamministries.com, if interested.

25. If life were found on other planets, how would this effect your belief system?

Supplement-1

WHAT IS A CHRISTIAN

To answer the question, one has to begin with what one can actually see, and that is man himself. Now, within man (in the generic sense which includes women) one can see a selfish core that seems to be inherited (Gen. 3, Rom. 5: 12, Rom 6:23, IJohn 1: 8, Rom 3: 23, and John 5: 17) . And man has to be cognizant of this fact and the fact that he needs help in following God's perfect law (I John 1:9-10, Ex. 20:1-17, and Duet. 5:6-21).

A more spiritual way in looking at this is that assuming God to be Perfect (Math 5:48 and Psalm I8:30), "How can a perfect being ever mix with an imperfect being to help the latter become obedient to the Perfect Being's law?". The only way that this relationship could be brought back together again, that is where perfection could be united with imperfection, is that the better state has to take the lead, since it is the stronger suit that is needed in initiating such a unification (I Cor. 13:10, and I John 4:19).

Christians believe that God did this in the person of Jesus Christ (John 3:16). They believe that Jesus came down to earth to identify with imperfection, mingled with humanity for awhile, sacrificed Himself for it on the cross, and returned to His original state (Perfection as part of the Trinity or God in relationship) through the resurrection (Romans 5:15-20).

In other words, Jesus Christ, who is also God (John 1:1-2, 14 and 17 and John 12:44-45) divested Himself of everything on the cross, which included all His power, all His possessions including all His clothes, and His life because of our separation from God or Perfection, and then was raised up (Math 28, Mark 16, Luke 24, John 20&21, ICor. 15) . To put it another way, He became pure imperfection for us on the cross before becoming Perfection once again (Romans 4:25).

Another way in looking at this is that those who are dependent upon and confess or admit this separation with this outside source, and believe in these activities of Jesus Christ (Christians) are now wrapped up in a state of Perfection, just like a Christmas package, to seal in our own imperfection (Romans 10:9-10 and 5:9-10). Not that we become perfect, but when God looks at His believers, all that He can see is the impenetrable outside wrapping, Jesus Christ, which in effect, is really like God looking into a mirror at Himself. And we, as believers, though remaining imperfect ourselves, but perfect inside Christ, grow, love more, and respond in more beneficent ways as our whole being is more and more immersed by this wrapping expanding and seeping into our hearts. In other words, our actions are determined by how much of His presence we have of Him within ourselves, and from this, love expands and there is a greater presence of the Kingdom of God here on earth. And the best way of bringing this presence of Him about here on earth is by praising Him individually, or better yet, in a group which is called the Church.

Supplement-2

WHO IS JESUS CHRIST

Who is Jesus Christ? According to Christians, Jesus Christ is the Son of God. He is also our Savior in that He saved us from our sin by suffering and dying on the cross and being raised from the dead. He was God's sacrifice for us. It was like perfection saving imperfection. But we actually have to believe in all this so that we can then become wrapped up in our belief, or Jesus Christ, just like a Christmas package, so that when God looks at us, all that He can see is His Son (perfection), or Himself as if He were looking into a mirror.

Now how do we know all this? By reading the Gospels. But how do we know that the Gospels are really trustworthy? To go into this, you have to look at the Gospels, not as the literal Word of God, but as historical documents. In doing this, you have to ask certain questions about these documents . 1) Do the documents portray eyewitness accounts? The Gospels do. 2) Do the documents contain irrelevant material not pertinent to the eyewitness accounts? Yes, they do. 3) Do the Gospels contain self-damaging material? Yes, they do. For example, the boldness of some of the women during this time period, and the statement Jesus made from the cross when He cried out" My God, My God, Why have You forsaken Me?" 4) Do all 4 Gospels have a consistency as well as a divergency in perspectives? Yes, they do. 5) Do the Gospels increase their legendary exaggeration? No, they don't, even though they do have some supernatural events in them. 6) Is there any indication that the writers of the Gospels have an ulterior motive for writing them? No, there isn't. In fact they could have faced persecution for writing them. 7) Can outside sources from that time authenticate the Gospels? Yes, they can and do. 8) Do archaeological findings substantiate many of the Biblical events related to us in the Gospels? Yes, they do. And 9) Were there many opponents of the Gospels at the time that could disprove the Gospels, but couldn't? Yes, there were. These are all questions that should be asked to determine whether a document has historical merit or not. And if the answers are all in the affirmative, except for questions 5 and 6, then the document has historical authenticity. In this case from the answers given above, the Gospels appear to be authentic historical documents and can be used as historical evidence for the life of Jesus Christ.

But there still seem to be many historical discrepancies within the Gospels. This actually can be explained away by realizing that the Gospels were never intended to be a biographical sketch of Jesus Christ, although there was much biographical material contained therein. The purpose of the Gospels was really to convey a message of salvation for the readers. In doing this, the discrepancies then become irrelevant.

And finally the authorship and date that the Gospels were written are not essential elements to the credibility as to what the Gospels actually say, although from the Book of Acts it does seem to say that at least the first three Gospels were written before 60 AD, and that the authorship of Luke is almost a certainty, whereas the authorship of the other Gospels are closer to a certainty than not. But the bottom line is that there is enough historical authenticity in the Gospels to make them worth-while reading.

Supplement 3

ABOUT THE BIBLE

What about the Bible? Can you believe all that you find in the Bible? But before this question is answered, you have to ask the question as to why God can't be more obvious in what He really wants from us? The problem here is that even if He were, we probably would want to do our own thing anyway. There are several reasons for this. 1) The impression stupendous events have on us, such as miracles, are never permanent and fade away with time. 2) There are always other explanations available for anything you observe. 3) Divine things are never as clear in this world because of the spiritual warfare going on around us. And 4) God only wants a loving trusting relationship with us, and this requires a moral decision by us, not absolute proof which would require no moral decision having to be made whatsoever. Besides, nothing is ever absolute.

Now getting back to the Bible. It's true that there are some unbelievable stories contained therein, but in a sense, you have to look at the Bible as a baby carriage carrying the baby, whereby the baby carriage can have many defects in it, while the baby cannot, although sometimes it's hard to distinguish between the two. Also many of these so-called defects are really not defects at all, but a way of making a point allegorically that couldn't be made more effectively in any other way. After all, the Bible is basically not an historical or scientific book, but a book to show us how we could be redeemed. Now if you consider the Lordship of Jesus as portrayed in the Gospels as authentic, you have to consider the Bible itself as being authentic, because Jesus uses so much of the Old Testament in His teachings. In other words, the Gospels' authenticity lends itself to the authenticity of the rest of the Bible. Besides the Bible seems to have a unity of purpose, despite the diversity of its authorship, because of its prophetic, and archaeological accuracy in many instances, and the Bible as a whole has given many people tremendous spiritual uplifts throughout the centuries. Therefore if you consider the Gospels as being historically authentic, you also have to trust the Bible as a whole in being historically reliable as well. But why so much violence in the Bible, especially in the Old Testament, whereby sometimes whole groups of people are killed under a loving God's direction? One has to realize that one has to measure one kind of evil against another, especially if the particular evil you want to stamp out is going to interfere with God's universal plan for redemption. Besides, you still have the after-life to sort out what's right or wrong.

But with one authoritative Bible, why do we have so many Christian denominations with different translations and interpretations of the Bible? There are basically 3 reasons for this. 1) Primarily because of the sinfulness of the church, in that, despite the fact that Jesus prayed for unity among His children (John 17), our pride and arrogance insisted on our divisiveness. It's amazing that Jesus can still minister through this sinful church. 2) Some churches view the authority of the Bible in different ways, such as the Roman Catholic Church which views the Bible, Church Tradition and the Pope as equal in authority, and the Fundamentalists who view the Bible simply as a Supreme Legal Document. And 3) some churches have honest differences of opinion on how to interpret different portions of Scripture, such as the role women should play in the church, due to the frailty of our human understanding. But the central message in all these traditions is still the same in that Jesus Christ died for our sins and saved all of us who believe in Him. And although the Bible is the prime source for this central message, God can speak to us in many other ways as well.

CHRISTIANITY AND OTHER RELIGIONS

THIS PAGE SHOULD BE USED TO WRITE ANSWERS TO THOSE QUESTIONS IN THIS CHAPTER IN WHICH YOU'RE INTERESTED. IF NECESSARY, USE ADDITIONAL PAPER.

Chapter 10

HOW ONE COULD LOOK UPON DEATH AND THE AFTER-LIFE

I'm sure you've experienced the death of some of your loved ones, but have you ever thought about your own DEATH and what it might be like if you feel that you're actually dying? Also what would you want put on your tombstone to commemorate your accomplishments during your lifetime? And is there an AFTER-LIFE? And what do you think the After Life might be like if there is one? Is there actual proof of an After-Life? And what activities do you think we might get involved in and who do you think you might meet in the AFTER-LIFE? I hope this questionnaire would start to answer some of these questions because this is where we are all eventually going to end up. And it also asks a question about the repercussions of what life would be like if you could live forever. Just try to answer some of the questions that seem pertinent to your life. .John 14:1-4, I Cor. 15:3-7, 12-19, Etc

Questions

1. What are the 5 basic stages of grief that one goes through when one loses a loved one, or for any other loss, and how do they operate?

2. Why do some people die so young? And why, even though we pray for their healing, some never get well, and continue to suffer and die?

3. Why do some during healing services get miracle cures, whereas others don't?

4. Today we tend to live longer. What would be some of the consequences if we could develop an indefinite physical life span? Would you enjoy this? How would this effect our relationship with time?

5. How would you relate to the death of a loved one? Could you relate to hospice (terminally ill) patients? How?

6. What would your continuing reaction be if you learned that your best friend had only 6 months to live?

7. Should you tell one that he or she's terminally ill? How? Would the patient know anyway?

8. What would your continuing reaction be if you learned that you only had 6 months to live?

9. Do you believe in life after death? Why or why not?

10. Are you afraid to die? Why or why not? If you are, are you afraid to live as well?

11. After you die, what do you want placed on your tombstone so people can remember what your life might have stood for?

12. What difference would it make in the life of others, if you had never been born?

13. What does Christianity teach us about death and what happens to us after we die?

14. Do you believe in a Hell, and if you do, who would go there? And what would Hell be like?

15. What do other religions (Judaism, Muhammadism, Buddhism, Hinduism, etc.) teach us about death and what happens to us after we die? How do these religions compare with Christianity concerning this matter?

16. What is Reincarnation and do you believe in it? Why or why not?

17. Do you feel that life is meaningless, or like chasing the wind, if you don't develop a relationship with God? (Read the Book of Ecclesiastes).

18. Do the near-death experiences that some people have, such as situations where most find a long dark tunnel, a light and music at the end of that tunnel, floating body experiences, etc., prove to you that there's life after death? Have you ever had a near-death experience which indicated to you such a happening? The author has had a floating body experience at the age of about 9 when knocked unconscious by a car.

19. Do parapsychological investigations (scientific research where they seem to have discovered a spiritual realm) prove to you that there's life after death? Have you ever had a parapsychological experience indicating the possibility of an after-life?. How does Christianity look at near-death experiences and parapsychological experiences?

20. Do you believe that there are some animals who have souls so that they can be saved too?

21. Do you believe in a purgatory? If so, what would be the purpose of a purgatory?

22. What do you think life after death might be like? Who do you think you might meet there? **Would this include all of your family even if some hadn't accepted Christ, pets, basically good people who are not Christians, immature children who can't accept Christ yet, retards, people who are mentally incompetent, suicide terrorists who feel they were doing it for God, Criminals who became criminals because of their parental environment, Parents of same, Christians who have hurt a lot of people in doing what they thought was the right thing, but wasn't, everybody, or psycho or sociopaths.**

DEATH AND THE AFTER-LIFE

THIS PAGE SHOULD BE USED TO WRITE ANSWERS TO THOSE QUESTIONS IN THIS CHAPTER IN WHICH YOU'RE INTERESTED. IF NECESSARY, USE ADDITIONAL PAPER.

_____

_____

_____

_____

_____

_____

_____

_____

_____

_____

_____

_____

_____

_____

_____

_____

_____

_____

_____

_____

_____

_____

_____

THE AUTHOR'S AUTOBIOGRAPHY AND HIS EXPERIENCE WITH JESUS CHRIST

I was born in New York City on May 6, 1931. My childhood was spent growing up on Long Island with a brother who was 5 years my junior and 2 loving parents. Although my father seemed a little bit distant from me, I seemed to inherit a love of sports and my sense of humour from him, and a compassionate heart from my mother.

Despite my inheritance from my mother, however, I grew up with a phlegmatic personality. This meant that I was quite shy, a loner, fearful of people, cautious, reliable, but never wanting to get involved, an observer of life, and usually did what I was told. As a result of this character mould, I was usually picked on by other kids which in turn made me even more fearful of other people. And my church experience at the time proved mostly negative, even though my parents were quite active church-goers, and I did feel rather close to God.

This phlegmatic personality stayed with me throughout my university career where I graduated from Roanoke College in Virginia with a B.A. degree in Political Science in 1954. I did, however, feel closer to the church, because most of my friends there were pre-ministerial students.

Four years after graduating from the university, I married for the first time and started going to church steadily a few months later where I probably became Born-Again. My vocation at the time was that of an accountant with a degree in same from LaSalle Extension University in Chicago. I was still a phlegmatic, however.

My transformation experience occurred when I visited a nudist camp a few years later which turned my life around 180° by giving me the freedom (no clothes), for the first time, to really be myself causing me to become a much more people sensitive individual. As a result of my new people concerned orientation, I received my Masters Degree in Religious Education from New York Theological Seminary in NYC in 1968, got actively involved in politics, started to organize discussion groups, started a jail ministry, and began many other people oriented activities. It is interesting to note here that as I participated in more and more of the nudist camp activities, I noticed less and less the nakedness (both male and female) of the individuals and more and more of their distinctive personality characteristics.

Eleven years after my marriage, my first wife died in open heart surgery. After this I went public with my nudist camp activity, principally thru my church, and the response was mostly positive among my close associates, although extremely negative among others. But people seemed to grow as a result of this disclosure. In fact, a professional writer used me as one of her positive characters in one of her books as a result of my disclosure. I also discovered that mentioning my nudist camp activities, opened others up to be much more honest with each other about their inner-most lives.

I married again four years later after the death of my first wife. She's Argentine. After about 8 years living in the States we moved to Argentina to be with my wife's family. In moving to Argentina, I basically gave up my accounting career and started teaching English to adults, which in turn developed into many business and personal counselling sessions, accelerated by my Stephen Ministry (counselling) training in Argentina. This turned out to be the greatest blessing for me, because I learned a great many things that I would never have learned if I stayed up in New York. In fact, I felt this type of job is probably one of the most important jobs one can ever have in the world, because the participants can learn much more about each other's culture than they otherwise would. But I also learned a great deal about the over-all business environment as well. This is what I've been doing most of the time that I've been in Argentina. Now I'm semi-retired and have written a book entitled "The Church Library on Christian Concerns and Solutions" which is published by Authorhouse and can be ordered through your local bookstore or online on Internet via (www.authorhouse.com/bookstore, www.amazon.com, www.barnesandnoble. com,) or on any other online website. The chapters in this book have already been published over Internet and have received a total readership of over 28,000 people.

At present, my greatest love, as far as ministry is concerned, is in the Ministry of Reconciliation. I have already done some of this in discussion group settings on Predestination, the Viet Nam War, the Purpose of the United Nations, with someone who was unjustly accused of being a communist, and in possibly helping my present church and its Board have better communication skills with each other. They were all quite successful. Now I hope this present book, which you can find the same way you might have found my first book, will serve the same purpose, and maybe this book could serve as a supplement or follow-up course to the Alpha course that is so popular among many of the churches. And I owe all this experience that I have had to my acceptance of Jesus Christ as my Lord and Savior earlier in my life.

Responses from the Internet church

1) That is a most fascinating glimpse of an autobiography, Corbin! I think, like many uptight English people, my eyes were caught by what you had to say about nudity. Wasn't it nakedness in the Garden that made Adam and Eve realise who they were? It seems to have happened to you. And so glad to hear that after a tragically early bereavement you found love and companionship again.

2) Thank You Corbin

3) Thank you Corbin, that was fascinating.

4) Thank you for sharing this Corbin, very insightful

5) Wow, what an awesome testimony !!! God can certainly use any situation and make a teaching out of it for us !!!